Accession no.

KU-743-280

That bad music is played, is sung more often and more passionately than good, is why it has also gradually become more infused with men's dreams and tears. Treat it therefore with respect. Its place, insignificant in the history of art, is immense in the sentimental history of social groups. *PROUST*

Make the most of the music
That is yours. *SONDHEIM*

LIS - LIBRARY

Date	Fund
04/03/19	xu-Shr

Order No.
02912533

University of Chester

In the Basement

Call it dumb, call it clever · Long before its kind was manifestly endangered, the Broadway musical took on a protective coloration. Thanks to the curious discursive exemption that it may have been alone among the forms of our mass culture in enjoying, the musical was already prevented—or perhaps spared—from being an object of serious thought. Its formal description had always been left to the handiwork of technicians and aspiring show doctors, and its history was no more likely to cease being written in playbill-style reminiscences than its sociology was to leave the bush leagues of a boosterism intent on pushing the American way. Yet, as if this general neglect were somehow not enough, at a certain moment—say, in 1943 with *Oklahoma!*—the Broadway musical came to seek misrecognition even in its own limelight, and all the heralded breakthroughs of its so-called golden age consisted in embracing with ever greater rigor the "dramatic model" of a show whose musical numbers, no longer introduced by pretexts as diaphanous as the hosiery on the female chorus line that was losing prominence in the same sea-change, now had to be strictly rationalized by the dramatic situation, which they had in turn the all but moral duty to advance. The musical thus let itself be colonized, or camouflaged, by the same narrative naturalism from whose tedium and tyranny its real merit was to keep alive, so long as it was vital itself, the prospect of a liberation. No doubt, we should all have been richer—less stupefied and better entertained—if the reverse procedure had been adopted, and instead of attempting to confer on *Oklahoma!* and its progeny the unremitting dramatic consistency of Clifford Odets or Arthur Miller, one had given to the work of the latter the formal structure of a Broadway musical, and so not only relieved us from its self-important earnestness but elucidated its latent sentimentality as well. But even as matters stood, the stranglehold of the dramatic model only better rehearsed the sense of suffocation that had always underlain the breathless pleasure that the musical, despite its new public relations, hadn't ceased to afford, but that had now acquired, through them, the more intense character of a secret.

Watch my dust · No one better appreciated the secret, or more passionately bore its defining paradoxes, than the kind of boy who, during the '50s, at the height of Broadway's golden age, descended into his parents' basement to practice the following occult ritual. Ensconced in this underworld where he was equally removed from company at home and the lack of it at school, he would pass a tentative hand into the recesses of a small chest; no sooner had he done so than, though New York City was nowhere near, the air suddenly filled with the din of songs from the latest Broadway shows. And his shamanism then began in earnest: to the strident storm thus raised, he would utterly abandon himself, now tapping furiously away (while in his stocking feet), now belting out a vocal accompaniment (albeit only mouthing the words), now breaking down into sobs (so moved he was by the bravery of his refusal to do so). However persistently his original cast albums had tutored him in the concept of the so-called integrated show, not all his ingrained docility could prevent him from laying claim to a counter-knowledge as defiant as any first act finale, for in the cheerless drama of his life beyond these confines, he too had reasons to want to stop the show, starting here, starting now. What he consequently sought in the Broadway musical was the very thing that those who despised it also found there: not the integration of drama and music found on the thematic surface, but a so much deeper formal discontinuity between the two that no makeshift for reconciling them could ever manage to make the transition from one to the other less abrupt, or more plausible. As often as it had numbers, every Broadway musical brought him ecstatic release from all those well-made plots for whose well-made knots no one who hadn't been a boy scout could possibly have a taste. The bliss was irresistible, for instance, when a team of inept baseball players broke into a song so hearty that it could have drowned out even those catcalls that must have followed had they ever performed it in the vicinity of a real-life diamond—when, in other words, a baseball story got to renounce the ethos of playing ball for that of just playing, or just bawling, like the boy in the basement himself. And so with the genre as a whole: its frankly interruptive mode-shifting had the same miraculous effect on him as on every character, no matter how frustrated in ambition or devastated by a broken heart, who felt a song coming on: that of sending the whole world packing.

Broadway baby · This effect is most copiously distilled in the show tune, that vehement hymn to self-belief which, albeit the least mistakably "Broadway" of Broadway songs, has been branded with the same restricted cultural mobility that every abashed provincial used to pray to the name of Broadway for help in overcoming. For unlike the song whose pretty melody and sweet-tempered lyric, so unobjectionable as to be considered striking, once let it march right

⟶

I'm calm, I'm calm, I'm perfectly calm · "In 1956, if you wanted to play a record on a hi-fi phonograph, you would first set it on a spindle, where it was held in place by a metal arm, and then push a switch to a setting marked 'Reject.' This caused the record to drop onto a turntable while a so-called stylus, attached to an arm of its own, having risen as the record fell, swung to the outer border of the latter's surface, and descended on it; at which point the switch moved of its own accord to another setting marked 'On.' The whole process was so visibly labored, and the various movements of it bore so audibly discontinuous a relation to one another that, even after I had mastered it, I would stand watch over it while it was being accomplished. For though, as the brochure said, these were simple controls that 'even a child can operate,' yet to what was purposeful in the aim of their movements was always added an uncontrollably arbitrary or acciden- tal character of execution, which might miscarry despite the best of intentions. Perhaps I was confusing this willing, but not quite reliable apparatus with the incompetent boy who ran it, and incurred the risk, if it malfunctioned, of getting into trouble, but it did often happen that things went wrong. The concussion of the falling record might dislodge the others stacked above it; and these would collapse onto the stylus arm, which in turn skidded suicidally across the record, damaging it before destroying itself. Or the stylus in descending might miss the record altogether, or miss its surface but not its edge, and be frayed by the re- cord's revolutions. Under such conditions, the music that eventually emerged was particularly wonderful, whatever joy it brought me on its own merits being associated with the relief of, for the time being, not having to worry about the machine."

ZENITH HIGH FIDELITY PHONOGRAPH

The BRAHMS Model HFY-17R

Model HFY-17R

out of the theatre into the hit parade, whence, become as old and devalued a standard as a film star working in television, it is now piped into shopping malls the world round, or the song that, possessed of wit as suave as a society escort's, only bared its soul ironically, the better to shield whatever vulgar or awkward importunities would have counted as bad form in the WASP world where, but for this wit, and also by means of it, they rest unexpressed—unlike either of these, the quintessential show tune, celebrate movement or extol the virtues of travel as it may, rarely gets further than the nearest piano bar from its Broadway origins, which in any case it lacks either the good looks or the educable manners to enable anyone to forget. Whenever, having first alloyed the tin of its orchestration, or the brass of its singer's chest voice, it shoves its bumptious way into the opera house, the concert hall, or even the supper club, it suffers humiliations as intimate as those of a body that has suddenly relinquished control of its functions; and even performed to thunderous applause on its own necessarily overprotected stage, it retains something of the contradiction that characterizes a flop in the tension of a spectacle that, despite being fully intended as such, is capable of embarrassing its spectators as profoundly as if they were witnessing a scene from which propriety demanded they avert their eyes.

Our leaders are cheerful · Its appointed mission—to deliver whoever sings it from disaster and dejection, from resentment, self-pity, and various other unconsoled relations to want—ought to make the show tune thoroughly at home in a society where, by means of a doctrine of "personal responsibility," authority likes to entertain the impossible dream of a population with nothing to complain about. For however manifold the misfortune, or complete the catastrophe by which I am overtaken, my stout rendition of the show tune entails my not having to suffer any of its consequences, psychic or otherwise. What matter if the external world tenders no better motive for my ascension over its wreck than that it has supplied the *prima materia* from which I may compose a small posy of my favorite things, when the real point of treating, say, poverty through exposure to the sun in the morning and the moon at night, or depression with, of all things, a little Christmas, is to exalt the performative power of a personal will that, even on such manifestly worthless external supports, remains potent enough to defy the hard-knock life by the simple decision to do so? But no amount of heart will keep the Senators' luck from batting zero— only the devil can do that—and on Fanny Brice's decree that nobody rain on her parade, there follows but more stormy weather. The elation of ego worked by the show tune is not just *voluntary,* having its source and sustenance nowhere outside a subject who pulls himself up by the tongue on his tap shoes, but also *vacuous,* too exhausted by the violence of affirmation to acquire any objective reality beyond its own thus belittled grand gesture. In the example that is most alert to this aspect of the genre, there is no longer even a nominal difference between the initial formulation of disaster ("They think that we're through . . .") and the terminal one of triumph (". . . and nothing's gonna stop us till we're through"), as though Rose unconsciously shared Sondheim's understanding that the true content of show-tune transcendence is simply the strength to endure a depressive status quo. That show tunes often ground this transcendence in some aspect of the mere act of performing them (whistling a happy tune, tapping your troubles away) exposes

the all but otherworldly asylum where the subject they rescue survives: in no business but show business. Accordingly, loudly brayed
independence proves indentured to the public relations of an indi-
vidualism that is indifferent and even antipathetic to sponsoring the
process, or legitimizing the effects, of actual individuation. In the
act of dismissing the world, the subject has so thoroughly accepted
his own dismissal as an agent in it, that the exhilarated spectacle he
presents of being "alive" is hardly distinguishable from a memorial
service conceded to him by the social order that, having just taken
him out of action, pays pious homage to his defunct vitality, the
better to claim, when it resumes its regular business, that it is doing
so in the very spirit of the deceased, who with his other great merits also happens to be the sort of person who would have wanted
one to "go on living": that is, to forget him.

They smile when they are low · Yet the show tune rhetoric
of denial is too brittle not to crack, and not to unmask through the
fissures the would-be invulnerable subject put to pasture in its Ely-
sian fields. The latter in fact has only been constituted to conceal—
or rather, by concealing badly, to disclose—a radically pathetic subject, who by letting us see that he is trying to hide his sufferings,
becomes additionally so. By a ruse as lubberly as the adolescents
whom the Broadway musical makes short work of recruiting to the
rank of its followers, his self-belief solicits our incredulity, and his
no less amazing self-sufficiency our support. "I am what I am, and
what I am needs no excuses," but this Yahweh-like claim gets retracted in every subsequent line of Albin's apologia, which does
nothing but badger and cajole the others he professes not to need

("*So what* if I love each feather and each spangle? *Why not* try to see things from a different angle?"), so as to extort from them the ovation that, by the time his consummate theatrical sense has inspired him to rip off his wig, fling it in Georges's face, and storm off the stage, down the aisle, and out of the theatre, there is no longer any doubt how much he prefers to the hook. All that the show tune finally achieves by its boisterous denial of suffering, therefore, is a certain vulgar "tact" in the latter's otherwise forbidden display. From this incipient breakdown of stoicism—a breakdown that threatens to spread via the mechanism of identification from the singer to his audience—stems the widespread cultural embarrassment with which Broadway music covers the ill-bred reluctance of personal need to become abstinence.

Sweetheart, they're suspecting things · Hence, only one thing is as common at the performance of a show tune as the fact that grown men and women surreptitiously take it on themselves to release the sobs they hear the performer stifling between the upbeats: namely, the fact that with far less inhibition, the same people celebrate the end of this disturbance with an ovation whose warmth they imagine to meet, not to say muzzle, her demand, and whose vigor persuasively shakes off whatever mollification the flow of those tears may have effected in their bodies. In a similar spirit of self-protection, on the nights of his civic light opera subscription, a certain style *père de famille* of the period used to rely on exhaustion and old-fashioneds to put himself into a torpor that would so completely keep him from knowing what was happening to him that nothing could happen; and his wife would only play the album

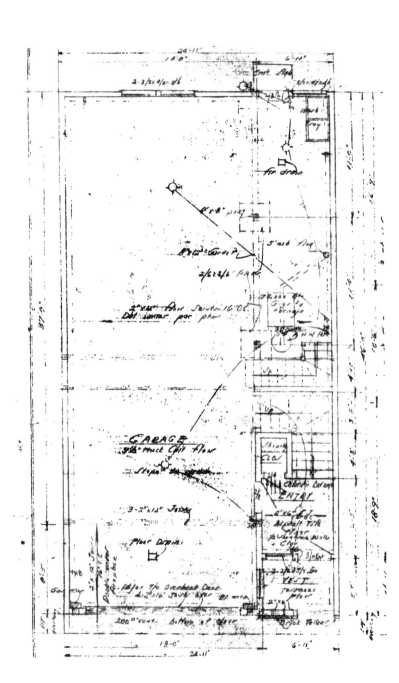

of *My Fair Lady* when he was out of the house. Nor was their son ever so overwhelmed by his passion that he forgot to manage the secrecy in which he indulged it, or if he did, if once when having moved his basement upstairs he was by some chance distracted enough to omit to draw the curtains on his performance, so that other boys in the neighborhood had been able to catch him in the act of vibrating sympathetically to the numbers that neither he nor they had ever seen, he soon understood—that is to say, too late— that his sense of embarrassment had been given to him, like the gag reflex in his throat, to warn against the social humiliation that must ensue if he were such a cockeyed optimist as not to heed it. (In the Alcatraz Island penitentiary, the prisoners' block was divided by a corridor from either side of which the new arrivals being escorted to their cells would be taunted and jeered at by those already incarcerated; this avenue of indignity bore the name "Broadway.")

◄————————————————————————————

Life down a hole · The archaeology of the post-war gay male subject regularly turns up a cache of original cast albums. These were used, scholars now believe, in a puberty rite that, though it was conducted by single individuals in secrecy and shame, was nonetheless so widely diffused as to remain, for several generations, as practically normative for gay men, as it was almost unknown among straight ones. The boys destined, as it was said, to be *musical,* would descend into the *basement* of their parents' home (see *Figure* left), and there they would sing and dance to recorded Broadway music (in one variant, merely mime singing and dancing) under the magical belief that, having lent the score the depth of their own abjection, they might then borrow all its fantastic hope that their solitary condition would end in glory and triumph. In contradistinction to other puberty rites, including their own, the only body fluids to pour forth in this one—but they did so copiously, orgiastically—were tears.

Another opening, another show · Hence, too, it is by no means true that, as someone says in *Applause,* "nobody loves a flop." The serious devotee of the Broadway musical has always been as much drawn to flops as to hits, barely bothering, perhaps barely able, to distinguish between them, as though his having a taste for the genre precluded his having any taste in it, and the detailed exposure required to make him a connoisseur had only succeeded in making him indiscriminate. Nor may this addiction to flops be convincingly put down to the savagery of enjoying seeing people fail. Such sadism merely belatedly encrusts, as a show tune does the suffering that no one is interested in hearing, his excruciated sense that these flops have spoken the truth of the Broadway musical, that for which he had originally cathected it, when, in the basement, as soon as he read the reviews, he took flops to his bosom with the same excessive affection that Louise showed one of her pets in *Gypsy,* no doubt sharing his opinion that, in this great show, "Little Lamb" was the only dog. Against all the odds of its oddness, he would root for a doomed show by making a daily tally of its consecutive performances till their total should at least have spared it extreme disgrace; and after it closed, he would no less superstitiously seek to keep it alive by playing to death its score, almost as though he were himself the bad idea, unworkable from the start, that, in the intolerable verdict of retro-analysis, no one or nothing could have saved.

I've got your number · Today, though, it has become part of the salesman's job to make you ashamed of asking for something so strange, old-fashioned, even indecent, as not to be part of his stock. In the satisfied tone with which he informs us, "I'm afraid we've stopped carrying that item for some time now," or inquires, "are you sure of the name?" he identifies himself with the plenitude of consumption refused only to those perverse enough to want what isn't provided, and who richly deserve all the contempt he is making sure they get. So too a similar type of man takes it on himself to enforce the embarrassing rhetoric of Broadway music by ridiculing it. Better than anyone this man grasps the depth and extent of its bad faith, whose ruses have met their match in the ingenuity of his ability to detect them. He is swift to spot the blackmail at the core of its emotional honesty, the self-importance that dictates its modest pretensions, or the inconsequence that belies its grandiose ones. When Albin professes to want to take "a little pride" in his world, this man will know enough to add, in his best Harvey Fierstein imitation, now, is *that* so wrong? Yet to charge this rhetoric with dishonesty is itself dishonest for refusing to recognize how little our social order likes to confront the suffering that is paying its installation costs. The rankness of bad faith supposes the availability of more direct, honest ways to express need, whereas everyone knows that the only socially credible subject is the stoic who, whatever his gender, obeys the gag rule incumbent on being a man. The declaration of all personal demand or desire tends thus to pass through the rhetoric of a person with nothing to declare, and therefore to bear a necessarily "hypocritical" or "sentimental" relation to it: "I don't mean to complain, but . . ." So, despite his malice, the Broadway baiter is a good citizen after all. When he derides the nasal Broadway singing voice, his real target is the whining that, perhaps ever since his childhood sinus condition, he has struggled to keep under control. Regardless of what is correct in his account of "cheap Broadway sentimentality," he can never propound it apart

from his eagerness to show that he knows how to entertain sentimentality on an even more frugal scale.

Look what happened to Mabel · Sooner or later, as if in
playing *Hello, Dolly!* he had been playing with an actual doll, it befell
every kid in the basement that he was changed into one of the Boys
in the Band (who indeed intimate their earlier incarnation when for
a happy moment they suspend their supposedly definitive sarcasm
to indulge in what, while no less effectively giving them away, far
more truly sounds the depths of their nature: the formation of a
chorus line). Nothing is more amazing than this metamorphosis,
which after whatever quantity of repetitions sufficed to establish its
regularity has ramified from *a boy like that*—whose diffuse sentimentality proved to have been rehearsing on its imaginary stage a
far more precise, but hardly less embarrassing sexuality—to alter
our sense of the Broadway musical itself, so much so that, as though
the facade of its general address were being gradually eroded by all

----------→

Scrapbooks full of me in the background · "Laurents' published book to the
contrary, in no actual production of *Gypsy* has Arnold ever played an accordion.
By the time *Gypsy* first opened in Philadelphia, thanks to the musical abilities of
the child performer in question, Arnold's original accordion had become a guitar,
and later in the Broadway run, both had been transformed into the figure (definitive for all later realizations) of 'Clarence and his classical clarinet.' But it was
with an accordion that, as a boy, I marched miserably into lodge halls to com-
pete—and lose—against girls who twirled a baton or precociously sang the
blues. And I was the right age for Arnold in 1961 when the national tour arrived
in San Francisco where, having been captivated by the show since the cast album
came out, I finally got to see it. In a word, I cannot escape this absurd, but
staggering thought: *I might have played* Gypsy!"

the tears it elicited from him and his kind, the dilapidated form is now getting acknowledged (like the artist whose fame reaches him in his dotage, or the dying prodigal whom his family at last forgives, knowing his sins can't be repeated) as a somehow *gay* genre, the only one that mass culture ever produced.

You're a queer one, Julie Jordan · —Unless more amazing than any of the above be the fact that, ever since the newly revised Dictionary of Received Ideas came out, no one is left to be amazed by it. To recognize the Broadway musical for one of "the signs," the stupefied audience of network television has become as competent as the professionally trained psychiatrists and literary critics to whom Tennessee Williams once threw a subtly flavored bone when he conveyed the "latent homosexuality" of a character by the fact that as a youth the sweet bird had sung in the chorus of *Oklahoma!* In the admittedly monstrous case that he isn't gay, the aficionado of the Broadway musical must resign himself to being thought so, or work as hard as Frank Rich to establish his improbable but true sexual orientation. Conversely, though not all gay men—nor even most—are in love with Broadway, those who aren't are hardly quit of the stereotype that insists they are, which appropriates their musical taste nonetheless by imposing on it the burden of *having to take a position* vis-à-vis the mythos of male homosexuality for which, if only in America, an extreme devotion to the musical theatre is a chief token. Accordingly, A, with no heart for this theatre, becomes as rabid in dismissing it as if someone were proposing to put a dress on him; B erects his indifference into the same politico-didactic virtue that he might boast of were he careless about what he wore, or haphazard in furnishing his apartment; and C, while admitting to some interest, is careful not to exaggerate it: he is also good at managing the sexual indiscretions of which he is now and again guilty so that they never endanger his relationship—of longer standing than many marriages, he will have you know—with his lover. Nothing is availed by any of this. Their very determination to do so must prevent A, B, and C from shaking the belief that, like it or not, they remain obsessed with the Broadway musical; and in repudiating *the homosexual type,* they merely become the well-classified, even classic specimens of *the homosexual typology* constructed in relation to him.

Cliché coming true · For D, who under false pretenses has only elicited these responses from A, B, and C so as to know whether, when they found out about him, they would still be his friends, matters are just as bad. The stereotype is hardly truer when it is accurate, and even having no desire to beat it, he makes an awkward join with it. As the archives conclusively show, not a single twelve-year-old boy was ever brought before a psychiatrist, or prayed to Jesus for help, on account of his collection of original cast albums, to which neither was there any need perceived to affix warning labels. The historical uniqueness of the Broadway musical among "the signs" consisted in the fact that it never looked like one: though eventually proving not a whit less indicative than those that were horrifically transparent from the moment they appeared, it involved (as much as if it had been written in invisible ink) considerable delay before its first inscriptions achieved legibility—legibility that in consequence was rarely greeted by anything but, as over the sudden strange suitability of terms as incommensurable as *Mame* and Mom, surprise. Yet if nothing could be more usual in a

society that imbues it with secrecy than that male homosexuality should engender frequent effects of surprise, neither is anything more typical of current discourse on the topic, in which the most prodigious information, the most astounding observation is ritually said to "come as no surprise," than that its producers should go out of their way to proclaim their (urbane, panic-stricken) immunity from these effects. Not only does a dread of being caught, not to say taken, by surprise where male homosexuality is concerned— which as matters stand can hardly be anything other than a dread of what will already have occurred—seem to incite the entire multiform social will to knowledge of an entity called "the gay man" (who must be tricked out in every dog tag with which he can be plausibly thought, or reasonably persuaded, to accessorize his desire), it also tends to put such knowledge, be it popular or academic, homophobic or progressive, in the service of a mere knowingness whose only aim is, by reducing him to a set of signs, to display, amulet-like, its own mastery in reading them. What need, then, to approximate the various stupidities (not just the boy's, or his parents', but the genre's and that of its cultural surround) that gave his experience, in the good as well as bad sense, its density? So those of us in whom his experience is still being lived remain *not far from where we were before:* feeling if anything more forsaken now that everyone knows what it signified than when no one did (for we shared in the ignorance as we cannot share in a knowledge that ignores what Barthes has called the "obtuse" dimension of the signi-

◄───

That's all there is to that · "In those days, our favorite musicals were (left to right) *The Music Man, Gypsy, The Sound of Music,* and *Carnival.*"

fier). Grudgingly accommodated, often hardly tolerated within the institutions and practices of a later-formed "gay identity"—with the major, but moribund exception that is the piano bar—this experience, all the more inner for having nowhere to come out, survives in only the most precarious form, at risk of dwindling down to a facetious convention, or of vanishing altogether into efficient social function, gay male division. In its sheer frailty, it requires what no purely theoretical or analytic language, but only a novelesque one, can give it: *demonstration.* (No less than Proust, Miss Adelaide wants "her memories in writing.")

•

When you're a Jet you stay a Jet · "In the cloakroom before the start of school, Wally would impress me into a brief, but tremendous game where, in lieu of a ball, I was knocked between him and his friends; whenever a floundering limb of mine so much as grazed his lower body, he would tell the others that my 'pervert hands' had attacked his 'privates.' But later in the day, during choral practice, knowing that Sister Emelda's piano seat held nothing better than fusty copies of 'Soul of My Savior' and 'You're a Grand Old Flag,' whereas my book bag was likely to be storing the bright red sheet music to *West Side Story,* lately made into a popular film, the same Wally would practically beg her to let the class sing these Vocal Selections while I accompanied on the Baldwin. Then, as in that miraculous intervention performed by the guardian angel depicted in my first catechism, androgynous creature whose winged support nullified all effect of gravity on his young charge as the latter was stepping unawares off a precipice, so on the simple, close harmonies of 'Maria' and 'Tonight' (to whose loveliness was added, in certain voices, a new note of good will toward me) I would be borne above the pull of dejection, whether exerted by Wally's cloakroom slander, or, ever since his outgrown uniform trousers paid out my first fat reward, by its truth. Yet to the harsh law that manacled my desire to my disgrace, so that, like partners in a slapstick routine, each must always be following the other's lead, show music offered no real exemption, nor would it have done so even if the other scores in my book bag had also been lucky enough to escape the censure of Wally and his friends. On the contrary, with its characteristic cross-braid of embarrassment and exultation, show music was what gave this law the widest permitted cultural expression. Absorbed into the camouflage of such publicity, my private griefs could seem to vanish, but in fact were so well preserved that just last week, at a performance of a show revived from my adolescence, the blithest songs being imbued as always with a discouragement, with a shame there was no shaking, I must break down into tears, the old ones I no longer had to keep from Wally.

Dames at sea · "As soon as I walked into his apartment, I saw them: several were just lying there on the floor, most with their jackets on, but a few in only those little white slips. As on the trail of a treasure hunt, one which hardly brought me pleasure and in fact seemed to eliminate the very prospect of any from my evening, my eye was led by the density of their distribution to the étagère where they assumed a form that was still more disturbing to me than all this overrunning chaos (which could, after all, be cleared away): namely, the abiding form of a *collection*. Overwhelmed, as by those perfumes about which one feels that, if they were anything

less than thoroughly nauseating, they might prove violently stimu-
lating, I found myself exclaiming: 'My God, you really *are* gay.' By
which I must have been expressing, not my amazement at the sexual orientation of my new friend, already established to my complete satisfaction, but my suddenly altered sense of his standing
within the gay milieu, as in a strange sort of swimming pool where
such acts of grown-up sex as we had been intending to perform
took place at the shallow end, with little danger that, from whatever positions we came to assume, we couldn't at a moment's notice recover our land legs, while the kid stuff like listening to
Broadway albums (arranged, as I later discovered, in a charmingly
idiosyncratic order) had required him to submit to a nearly total immersion in what my first phobic ejaculation confirmed was
pretty deep water.

Wise men never try · "I once gave a tape of *South Pacific* to a
man with whom I was secretly in love. It reproduced all the surface
noise of the LP, in my possession since childhood, from which I
had recorded it, and I was perhaps counting on the fact that the
noise became most distracting during 'Some Enchanted Evening'
(on account of my juvenile concentration on that particular band)
to break my silence with a declaration. On the following day, as he
thanked me for the music, with an even politeness that to my ear
couldn't help diminishing the 'great enjoyment' professed by his
words, he added with a laugh, as between friends who shared exactly the same viewpoint on things: 'How awful, though, to end up
some old queen in a piano bar watering your drink every time they
played "Some Enchanted Evening"!' Would it have done me any

good if I had known at the time—what I did not learn until several years later—that by his own account he had burst into 'hysterical sobbing' as soon as, through my good offices, he heard the very first bars of the song for which, a day after, he would convey to me his thorough contempt? As strange as it seems, I had always had a presentiment that my gift, on which I set great hopes, would prove futile. For I was attempting to impart to him that *homosexuality of one* which—even had he accepted it, or were himself to return the favor—must have restrained either of us from ever joining the other across a crowded room. The proper use of 'Some Enchanted Evening' was not, I concluded, and never could be, to court another man, whom hearing it would only return to the archaic condition where one dreamed all alone—like me, as I replayed the song 'again and again' after the still wonderful guy had gone.

Funny, isn't it? · "No matter how often during the specifically gay activities of my life—in a bar, at the gym, on the cassette player of a new friend's car—I encounter the Broadway musical, I find myself *surprised*. I am like those tabloid readers to whom the shock caused by a scandal is never diminished by the discovery they have made of the identical scandal only last week and never mitigates the blow they will receive when this same scandal is reheated for them next week. However intimately or indisputably knit into the stuff of my gay life, the Broadway musical never seems of a piece with it, but stands out in discontinuous, 'paradoxical' relief: as though it were perfectly ordinary that I, of all people, should frequent the company of men wearing weight belts, or nipple rings, and utterly strange not only that I should still be hearing music I have known since I was a child, but also that there should be others, many of these men among them, in the same strange situation as myself. In short, I am *committed* to this incongruity, to preserving it even to the point of cultivating its characteristic effects, as when, thanks to my walkman, I make all the bodies in the Muscle System move to the busy rhythms of an overture, or in obedience to the stringent bark of Ethel Merman.

If he walked into my life today · "An ex-boyfriend had the exasperating habit of suddenly 'for old time's sake' paying me an unexpected call. At first I would be astonished, almost charmed, by the naive vanity that could lead him, at this date, to presume on his welcome, as though ever since he had last disappeared, I had done nothing but wait eagerly for his return. I would also nearly gape at his unchanged, but now antiquated look, and casting a glance at the web belt whose excess length he still let dangle over his fly—a flirtation that, because I no longer responded to it, had become grotesque—I would think with pity: look at him, still stuck in the period when we met, whereas I . . . but the sentence only managed to get completed thus: *will never get over him.* Similarly, every time I hear the outworn Broadway sound, it is still mindlessly singing of that transcendental longing which I can never be sure whether I have outgrown, or (as I did this boyfriend, who on the rare occasions when he wasn't less, was so much more than satisfactory) merely renounced."

Be sure that you lock up your wife and daughter · As a youth, the sweet bird had sung in *Oklahoma!*

She's too close for comfort · In the psyche of post-Stonewall man, the Broadway musical lies like a nervously watched pod that, having been preserved from a past geological epoch, may nonetheless—say, at any temperature above frigidity—split open to reveal a creature that, in comparison with the less primitive forms of life around it, even with those which must have evolved from it, will appear monstrous beyond recognition. Along with very few other terms (for example, in a tongue the author knows less well, "Barbra Streisand"), "Broadway" denominates those early pre-sexual realities of gay experience to which, in numerous lives, it became forever bound: not just the solitude, shame, secretiveness by which the impossibility of social integration was first internalized; or the excessive sentimentality that was the necessary condition of sentiments allowed no real object; but also the intense, senseless *joy* that, while not identical to these destitutions, is neither extricable from them. Precisely against such realities, however, is post-Stonewall gay identity defined: a declarable, dignified thing, rooted in a community, and taking manifestly sexual pleasures on this affirmative basis. No gay man could possibly regret the trade, could do anything but be grateful for it—if, that is, it actually were a trade, and his old embarrassments (including that of whatever gratification he was able to find through them) had not been retained, well after the moment of coming out, in the complex, incorrigible, rightly called fatal form of character. Wherefore, the Broadway musical develops for many a gay man into that contradiction in terms, a *living relic:* it must be granted existence (unlike the photographs of his body before he started working out), but only a shady one, tucked away in the closet, where cast albums and playbills occupy the space vacated by the recent removal of the erotic accessories to beside the bed. (In *Longtime Companion,* Fuzzy feels obliged to conceal the moment of recidivism, when, with the cast recording of *Dreamgirls* blaring, he performs the title song before a mirror, even from his lover, whose sudden arrival stops the show cold. AIDS now seems added to the reasons for repression—as though Fuzzy had no right to sing "life's not as bad as it seems" when it is plainly so much worse, and this trope of the show tune were not any less evocative of sorrow than is, in gospel music, amazing grace.) Judging from the attitudes that post-Stonewall man adopts to cope with it—attitudes that make it at best a pleasure permitted only on condition of melancholy or ironic discretion, and otherwise a taste so bizarre as to deserve, or so seductive as to demand, nothing short of stigma—we should never think that this unavoidable, but unwanted presence in his midst was the same bosom buddy who used to take him along on countless trips to New York, New York, an even more wonderful town, if possible, than the city of strangers whose company in later life he would get off of the train to seek; to whom he was also indebted for his first serious instruction in wordplay, which, not least when he was enjoying it entirely for its own sake, always answered the expressive purpose of taking him to and fro between some version of *hellish* and some version of *swellish;* on whose arm, down the cul-de-sacs of his youth, as he talked to the trees that didn't listen to him, or smelled blossoms when they were bare, he never walked alone, and to this day, whatever the form of the storm that may brew, when the love light is fading in his sweetheart's eye, or he is sick of having a sick world, he continues to lean—we should never think, in short, that the thing now under his chill, compulsive surveillance was the Broadway musical; on the contrary, we should have taken it for what the general culture around him persecutes and tolerates, in just such ways, as his own homosexuality.

At the Bar

And no one cares how late it gets • No place better realizes his juvenile dream of grown-up space than this piano bar: where he produces so many signs of adultness that one would almost think he is suffering from a delusion that (despite his frequent patronage or his manifest majority) there may even now arise some difficulty about his right to be here, which he is prepared to assert by exercising it in every way possible. As he inhales the intoxicating bitterness of adult life through the tobacco, or imbibes it in the alcohol, whose prodigal consumption starting from the moment he gets past the door only the eagerness of his intemperance persuades us is not a formal condition of admission, like the removal of one's shoes in a Japanese foyer, he is celebrating not so much how far he has journeyed from a place—his mythically straitlaced home or home town—as his distance from a time, that of his childhood, when he couldn't abide either of these acrid tastes. And if it were not enough that the law had already designated both substances for adults only, he must further subject them to protocols connoting adult ways of consuming them. Well versed in the manual of sophisticated smoking, for instance, he pinches the cigarette tensely between thumb and forefinger, as though held with any less rigidity it would be in danger of slipping from his grasp, or even of disintegrating, while his remaining fingers, left to fend for themselves by the motor exertions this vise requires, fly ungovernably into the air. So he means to signify the adult theme of Work, having understood from his father, who even off the job never had time for him, that smoking, only apparently allied with the conditions of leisure, relaxation, pleasure, was really of a piece with all those worrisome, demanding obligations of adult life that, unlike a child who "didn't have to" perform them, but had only to hear how indispensable the driven performance of them was to putting clothes on his back and a roof over his head, couldn't be neglected. Or, adopting the pose shown on a different page, he sets the cigarette stiffly at arm's length behind him or to his side: by which gesture he burns incense to adult Self-determination, the triumph of his will to smoke— or not—as he pleases, when—but only when—he wants. If "the habit" now makes that victory wholly imaginary, he is at any rate free of the asthmatic manifestations that formerly would have greeted the faintest wisp of one of those great clouds amid which, comfortable as a rococo divinity reclining on them, he now sits perched atop his stool. Or again, having turned another page, he waves his cigarette in so generous an arc that he might be a conjurer and it his wand. From the ashes that he scatters no less grandiosely than if they had come from the cinerary urn of a loved one, what is reborn is himself, a big boy now: this gesture of Largesse having literally secured his enlargement by the simple expedient of doubling the amount of space that others must allow him. The ingestion of alcohol (as distinct from its application, in the form of cologne, where mere proof of use is required) has similarly to bear the supplementary mark of sophistication, here inscribed by the fanciful nomenclature of *the cocktail,* that once mystifying set of names which he can never now pronounce without taking secret pride in the worldly initiation that has entailed their correct usage, or—what is the same thing—without feeling deep relief, whenever he orders a "screwdriver," a "grasshopper," a "greyhound," a "Manhattan," that the bartender does not scowl, or smirk, or give any other sign of being asked to bring forth from his shaker a tool, an insect, an animal, the whole metropolis.

Somewhere between forty and death · Having long ago passed out of its heroic age (if it ever knew one), his body now presents a gruesome phantasmagoria of the middle-aged male body in hell—being resistlessly tortured under demon architects who add hideous new wings onto the graceful old structures of belly and waist; demon engineers with pulleys that drop first the ass, then the jaw; demon artists adept at doodling lines across the face and distressing the canvas of the skin; demon hairdressers so cruel that they dye hair gray, or thin it out, give it a tonsure, even remove it altogether, while feigning to make amends for such depredations by inserting tiny thick toupees in ears and nose. And in their midst, a vengeful she-devil, smarting from gender oppression, is busy resculpting this body into a female one, rendering it mammiferous and broad—so her victim cries out—*where a broad should be broad,* and daring to recess, by this new disposition of mass, the cock itself! Yet he is not particularly dejected—not here, at any rate—by the fact that he is out of shape. On the contrary, the garment de rigueur on his upper body—a luxurious sweater (variously cashmere, alpaca, handwoven, brightly colored, "designed") whose full falling drapery, only pretending to wrap the trunk in a veil of mystery, shall faithfully imitate the thickening, slackening, and pleating of the flesh beneath, or whose snug fit, causing it to "ride" up the back or at the sides, shall directly expose these processes to view—flaunts pots and handles with as little modesty as the plain white T-shirt, more binding than a hair shirt but likewise bespeaking a discipline of iron rods and fasting, displays the gym rat's cuts and ripples. For just like a cardigan (or a blazer, or a foulard), his body too is an element of the dress code required by the celebration of adulthood here in progress. Hence he is disposed to wear it in the condition of Maturity, as the body of a parent. Only having "let himself go," evidently, is he entitled to assume the equally manifest condition of being free, light, airy: the body of a child.

I talk to them all in vain · With the same unshrinking determination that another kind of man might evince in scarifying a too delicate pair of hands, he has sacrificed the natural beauty of his face to its vivacity of expression. Instead of having a face, he makes them; and though his features are good, they never repose long enough for their owner to be held good-looking. On the contrary, they are always busy rolling, darting, tilting, arching, narrowing, puffing, flaring, puckering, biting, and otherwise assisting a discourse that, on the part of a man to whom language comes fast and fluently, seems curiously unsure of its ability to be understood. Not enough, in ordinary conversation, to entrust his point to overstatement, repetition, an emphasis of inflection; in addition, it must be captioned by a grimace that would make it literally as plain as the nose and other parts of his face. What would be his despair if he knew that his interlocutors accept his communication (provided they do) only after they have voided the whole violent drama of its performance—when, with every improbability corrected, every excess reproportioned, all that is left them to consider is some platitudinous "grain of truth" whose sheer familiarity condemns such unnecessary fanfare still further? Yet of course it is precisely out of such knowledge that there descends over his face, even to the point of somewhat muffling his speech, that spirit of self-negation which (perhaps mindful of the lifted eyebrow that is its symbol, or of the tension that it breathes into the other features as well) every beholder calls *archness*. For, as if these features were not sufficiently busy realizing the hyperexpressive intention confided to them, they simultaneously take on the extra burden of ironizing it: embedding within all its signs other signs that make it impossible to take straight, and so solicit the marginalization that it will be accorded in any case. Small wonder that so lively a face often looks "tired," exhausted by the exorbitant muscular expenditures to which the intuition of their futility has only added; or that so theatrical a face sometimes acquires an inscrutable air, having chosen to withhold what it can't give away.

Dis-donc donc donc donc donc · Yet almost as, on that other man, the hand gnarled in a long course of sores and injuries appears ugly until we see it exercising the craft responsible for its deformation: when, patently warranted by the work whose demands have shaped just this tool, it assumes such nobility that we are seized with an almost religious desire to kiss it, as if it were bearing stig-

mata; so, no sooner does this man join the choristers at the piano, and sing with them the Broadway songs that are the only music played here, than his absurd face, with all the contradictory agitations that were making it illegible, achieves point and poignancy in the same long breaths. Like old bits of rubbish transfigured by the significance they acquire from having been the implements of an ancient rite, the looks and tones before without rhyme or reason are now necessitated as the requisite mediations—or simply the inevitable consequences—of a practice as central to the piano bar as any rite can have been to an antique cult. And though this practice consists of nothing more than putting the words of songs into a certain vocal italics, the metamorphic force of the latter is so radical that, whether being putatively sung in the Middle Ages or the South Pacific, by a courting cowboy or a cloistered nun, every lyric now becomes a figure for present-day metropolitan homosexuality, which no lyric has ever cared, or dared, literally to mention.

'Stead of treated we get tricks · Thanks to this cataclysmic reformatting, Lancelot claiming "Had I been made the partner of Eve / We'd be in Eden still" no longer amazes Camelot with his chastity, nor does Eliza wishing "I could have spread my wings / And done a thousand things" remain angelic or even female. And when in the den of her fellow thieves, Nancy remarks "pockets left undone on many a behind," the "fine life" being celebrated no more concerns picking pockets than the "trouble" worked up by Harold Hill in River City—or for that matter the "Boys' Band" supposed to stave it off—bears on playing pool. "Adelaide's Lament" (since not just single words or lines, but whole songs may be set in these italics) is revamped for the role of a heartbroken queen, and "I'm

Still Here" for that of an old one. The heterosexual griping loses its grip on "Dames," as does the heterosexual gratitude on "Thank Heaven for Little Girls," where without them what little boys would do is now a question with an answer. And so, effortlessly, on. In the ease and immediacy of gaying up the repertory there isn't spared even the notion of a song that could not release, thus rubbed, a gay genie who had always been lying cramped inside it, but now wafts vaporously, to more or less mischievous effect, over every line.

Someone may be laughing · No matter that their few obsessive points and strategies of attack, which may be grasped in a minute, are rehearsed for hours at a stretch, the genie's antics never lose their power of being, to everyone present, hysterically funny. Strangely, though, even as these are in full swing, they disclose a melancholy whose ubiquity in the atmosphere, if always sensed, has until now remained as indistinct, as discreet, as that of the dust on the velvet drapes, or the grease stains on the old club furniture. Just as what Mame coaxes "right out of the horn," revivifying us in the process, is only the blues, so the practice that is channeling the patrons' high spirits into fits of hilarity would bespeak less a desire to *clear* the brooding air—for which such places, especially over the faces of their patrons, are of course well known—than the thrill of drawing from it a certain illumination, of (in the root sense) *elucidating* it. At moments—say, when the genie plays such havoc with a Rodgers and Hammerstein medley that the stranger you see across a crowded room is only that evening's trick, and Ado Annie's irresistible "Romeo in a sombrero and chaps," having left the range behind with his silly hat, looks as if he were ready for the Black

Party, perhaps to meet, during another song, someone from Austria older and wiser, telling him what to do—at such moments, the melancholy seems lit up as the irony of a practice that can only know itself as derivative and deviant. For unlike the aboriginal dandy who puts Western coins to the purpose of dress with supreme indifference to how they are used, or how his own use of them is viewed, in the civilization of their source, the allegorist of the piano bar, having been raised on the Broadway musical, is too thoroughly cognizant of the intended meanings of a lyric not to be equally so of the absurdity that would be charged against his double entendres, not to mention the contempt that would rain on them, if they ever left the shadows of what he also bears in mind therefore is no more than a subculture prevailed over by the culture at large. So deeply operative in him are the effects of that imagined wider circulation that they have been shaping all along a practice that makes up for the insolence of producing gay meaning by the courtesy of producing it *as nonsense,* in defiance of not just established interpretations, but even established principles of interpretation. He may not shrink before spoiling the loveliest song with his preposterous readings, but in doing so neither does he omit to call attention to their factitiousness and hence his powerlessness to offer them *for real.* It is as though he could not conceive of truth, beauty, reason, meaning, value, except as the exclusive properties of the mainstream cultural order that he thus lets condemn him— that he thus lets us know condemns him willy-nilly—to a trivial aberrance.

Peppered with actual shepherd · Yet at other moments, say, when the genie transforms Madame Rose into a momma's boy's momma, and West Side delinquents into Village deviants (but lets Bosom Buddies remain sisters); when he lends an outsider's animus to the satire on "the little things that make marriage a joy" in *Company*, or stands idly by, as though to say "it's all right with me," while a lyric (like the one to the song of that title) does his job for him— now, his work of appropriation doesn't seem all that inappropriate. Now, indeed, it becomes work of an altogether different kind: an archaeological excavation that unearths a joint between these gay meanings and the received ones that, contrary to previous impression, oddly appear to be based on them, like a medieval church laid on the foundation of a razed pagan temple, or an archaic palace erected over a still older place of sacrifice of which the people had grown ashamed. It is not that gay men are denied access to the sphere of cultural origination, but that as the price of admission they must surrender all right to being *recognized* in this identity, which now seems responsible for the melancholy of the place, for the irony of a practice that is bearing witness to an intimate, fundamental, and even spectacular truth about the Broadway musical that may nonetheless not be told on the legitimate stage—may not be told anywhere, for that matter, but here, in this shabby-pretentious ghetto bar, where it must be as overstated as everything else about the man to whom its revelation is entrusted.

Anyone can whistle, that's what they say · For like a third-rate magician who, thinking to take advantage of his inferior talent for illusionism, devises a novelty act in which he gives away the familiar tricks of his betters (disappointing all the same the general public that feels deprived of former delight along with former deception), this man is out to betray the habitual prestidigitation of the whole enormous population of gay composers, lyricists, librettists, choreographers, and others who, dexterously striking the sexual specificities of their experience with the wand of worldly ambition, cause these to evaporate into a cloud of nuance so diffuse and elusive that only the additional sleight-of-hand of a feigned tokenism can ever recondense it into representation. Indispensable to his treachery, therefore, is his complete somatic compliance with the stereotype of himself. It is thanks to this abandon that the homosexuality visible on stage only in the wake of its perpetual displacement acquires a legible, an undeniable body, one whose variously hysterical palpitations, keeping time to the music that sets them going and that they echo and amplify with brazen fidelity, manifest a link that theatrical production is—well it might be!—tireless in glossing over. With all the unanswerable impertinence of a poor relation or a spurned friend, he thus solicits recognition from a genre whose arriviste pretense of not knowing him, or whoever else might be shirking the heterosexual obligation romanticized in its old-fashioned weddings and pajama games, the spectacle of his unmatched familiarity with even its minor specimens shall unmask, and whose frequent winks of apology for this slight his overready comprehension shall deprive of all tact, so as to demonstrate beyond a doubt that the most distinctive historical mission of the musical theatre that everyone hummed was to give expression to those who, like him, couldn't whistle.

Smoke on your pipe and put that in · But this proposition, which his whole practice is dedicated to affirming, has no social standing or support outside it. For what could be particularly gay about any representation at a time when, on penalty of demonization, nothing particularly gay was allowed to enter it? And, even now, what kind of evidence could establish this particular gayness in a culture where, homosexuality remaining a quasi-criminal charge to be "proven," doubt will hasten to fortify any room, however infinitesimal, that is left for it to occupy? Just think: the golden-age musical that best persuaded the general public of the artistic "seriousness" of the form—and did so, naturally enough, on the basis of a virility so sure of itself, or at any rate, so truculently put forward, that it could even get away with the *jetés* of classical ballet, without anybody daring to say, though anybody might have seen, from their first cigarette, that the Jets were leaping straight out of the pages of Genet—this was entirely the conception of four gay men who must have been, in a strict sense of the phrase, nothing if not brilliant. By contrast to the opera, or Bette Davis movies, or any other general cultural phenomenon that enjoys, as we say, a gay *following*—in other words, that gay subjectivity comes to invest only after a creation at which it wasn't presumably present—the Broadway musical, with "disproportionate numbers" of gay men among its major architects, is determined from the inside out by an Open Secret whose fierce cultural keeping not all the irony on a show queen's face can ever quite measure, nor all his flamboyance of carriage undo.

I hear singing and there's no one there · Hence, from the labors of so improbable, so unprovable an argument, he will sometimes need to repose in the experience of self-evidence. Haunting all the adult practices in the place, there has always been a specter of regression for which, even as their sophistication would strive to exorcise it, their self-destructiveness or their silliness was serving as medium. And more than elsewhere such regression abides in the choral singing that, while essential to the very notion of the piano bar, is totally devoid of the grown-up quality suggested by smoking a Dunhill, drinking a Black Russian, or wearing a Corgi, and without these coefficients, would frankly recall the Sunday boys' choir, the bus to summer camp, or the high school spring musical. Sometimes, then, as soon as he joins the chorus in "Oh, What a Beautiful Mornin'!" or "Tonight," his countenance not only sloughs the strain of the years, so thoroughly in fact that his full mustache, his graying temples, the crow's feet at his eyes, and the deeper lines around his mouth (all of which of course remain) appear as foreign to his true expression as if they had been the result of an accident, or a concession to the surrounding masquerade, but also throws off the grip of youth itself, in the form of that habitual muscular concentration with which, as a child, he learned to belie the perturbation of his features, and so established the (smiling or serious or just blank) mien of rigor mortis that he still assumes against being looked at. The activity of singing—in this, reinforced by the anonymity of membership in a chorus—retracts him deep into a womb where what may be called his social physiognomy disappears along with every trace of his usual busy campaign to promote this or that of its aspects, and whence he seems as ageless as we do in the self-portraits we draw while asleep. Even when, small or strident, untrained or outright ruined, his song is not sweet to hear, the sight of how intimately he is given over to it—so much so that we can hardly avoid thinking he is pouring his soul, or singing his heart out—retains the potential to be ravishing in the extreme. (Lacking the better bodies, the piano bar will never be short on dreamy faces.)

Somehow, someday, somewhere · During the course of singing, for no reason he would ever be capable of giving, sudden tears
drop from his abstracted eyes, or he catches his breath in the middle of a line just as though he were heaving a sob, or practically
gasping for life. Like a half-witted docent sufficiently informed to
gather us before the most significant paintings in the gallery, but too
ignorant to tell us why we are pausing *here,* his voice is escorting
him through the master-episodes of youthful suffering, seldom recalled with much precision or in any detail, and often lost to narrative reconstruction altogether, but nonetheless known "by heart,"
thanks to the music that long ago combined with them as closely—
and now evokes them as inevitably—as if they had been so many
verses. Yet the voice that is thus always poised on the verge of
breaking down never actually does so, or only does so for a moment, when in any case its spasms are covered over by lost boys
(and Wendys among them) singing on different schedules of remembrance. All the faltering only seems to renew its determination to *sing out*—one might suppose in response to La Merm's in-
arguable command—and as it quavers and pants its way through
what accordingly becomes a kind of race against its own threatened
extinction, so exalted is it by the nearness of victory (to claim
which it merely needs to keep singing) that, albeit dependent on
the same old lungs and larynx, it all of a sudden miraculously out-
reaches itself, to achieve a volume, sustain a note, scale an octave,
undertake a counterpoint or harmony, forbidden to its powers but
a minute before. In the process of this prodigious enhancement
(whether having a real basis in his at last relaxed vocal cords, or
being only a subjective or group fantasy that a recording could easily contradict), the suffering he revisits is raised to ecstasy, as

though while recalling them, his voice could also at last proclaim the shadow-truth of those former moments of misery, which lay simply and even stupidly in his demand for, as it was called, the *happiness* in the tune. For, compared to when he would sing and dance to cast albums in the seclusion of the family basement, hearing in them a more particular address than the general one that elsewhere drowned it out, but never guessing that his secret audition was (wherever the Broadway musical flourished) so utterly normative that every urban gay community had institutionalized it in a bar like this one—compared to then, such utopianism, without exactly being gratified, has become so far less abstract that once whispered solos are booming forth in chorus.

I'm ready to move out in front · In that sense, the purest pathos here would belong not to the performer, but to the lost soul who, despite the fact that he has spent his entire visit wishing to take his place with the others at the piano, must bitterly reprove himself afterwards for at no point having overcome sufficient shame to do so: not at the start of the evening, when the paucity of witnesses ought to have given him confidence, nor at the height of it, when his inadequacies would have been concealed in the collective swell, nor even—most unaccountably—just before closing when, in the general sloppiness bred of drink and the hour, everything was lawful, vocally speaking. He is right to be depressed, for no one who has not sung along really understands what a piano bar is, or does; and by not singing, he has only made what it is and what it

Michael Perelman, *Only the Lonely*

does more loathsome—and needful—to himself than ever. Which is also to say, to ourselves, that no account of the place—not the ethnographic description of a symbolic practice, the psychological portrait of a human type, or the political rehabilitation of an unrecognized activism—is better than worthless unless, by recourse to autobiography or the novel, it finds a way to join the type in his practice for a few old favorites. (But what way? As the author has no voice—and even if he did, he would be obliged to lose it to his text—he will write what he never or no longer sings.)

•

"I FEEL PRETTY" · "What salve the lyrics of this song— had I ever sung them—might have applied to the tendency of my face in those days, whenever I imagined anyone looking at its imperfections, to burst into flames! What strength the rhythms of this song—had I ever danced to them—might have pumped into my then weakly body, which always drew a plenitude of vital force from treading to triple time ever since my mother used to waltz me around the dance floor of divers picnic grounds, and must have been additionally invigorated here where, by means of certain flourishes in the orchestration, that euphoric tempo was deliciously linked to the Latin dances made known to me at a somewhat later period by an even more beautiful woman who, in preparation for Arthur Murray or for some party or nightclub where couples got to exhibit the results of their apprenticeship at his Studio, had put on, instead of the print house dress she wore to picnics, a black sheath with earrings and sometimes a hat, and after telling me to stand up straight would initiate me into the formalities of, say, a

samba routine, in which we soon abandoned 'the basic' for crossovers and progressions, shuffles, spins, dips, then double or pivot dips; making arches of our hands and scissors of our feet, as with gradual recklessness we proceeded through a series of still more complicated figures called the Gaucho turn, the Tijuana twirl, the Miami walk, and the Cuban kick; even, to signify how far our dissipation had reached, breaking into a riotous double time from which we would nonetheless eventually relapse to convey the equally requisite after-effect, as we thought, of languor.

Send for Chino · "But in the repertory theatre in my parents' basement, solitary and secret though it was, an inflexible censor had banned 'I Feel Pretty' from all performance. He did so with the same staunchness that had decided him a few years earlier, after my first attempt at playing baseball, to prohibit any subsequent attempts, for he knew (being none other than myself) that having many of the talents, but none of the courage required to be a sissy, I could never be sufficiently sheltered from the opprobrious accusation of femininity unless I not only never risked the public malpractices that would invite others to hurl it at me faster than the hard ball I was too fearful to catch, but also abjured the private pleasures that would have compelled me to grasp it—instead of that hard ball—as my truth. Yet whereas his interdiction against playing baseball never stimulated the slightest interest in the game, that against performing 'I Feel Pretty' resulted in a close attention to the song that was all the more fervid for being silent and stationary, as though, like the eager foot-tapping of an invalid whom his physical condition alone confines to the side of a dance floor, my rapt listening were seeking—had even found—some compensation for the spectacle I wasn't allowed to make of myself. For during this sort of trance, I imagined that my wish for a place in the song was eventually granted by the lyrics themselves, whose concluding piece of wit seemed to suggest that they too were surreptitiously obsessed by the desire, so disapproved socially as to be all but impossible semantically, for a male prettiness, a male femininity. *For I'm loved / By a pretty wonderful boy!* Far from taking Maria beyond her narcissism (which he could no sooner do than shatter the mirror before which she presumably continued to sing) this 'pretty wonderful boy' simply refigured it—and to that extent, refigured Maria herself—in his image. No doubt, a grammatical equivocation took care to disown the prodigious conjunction to which, with all the ingenuity of a dream, or of writing under censorship, it thereby gave expression: where pretty-the-adjective conferred feminine graces on the boy, pretty-the-adverb (idiomatically, the more likely construction) threw the acid of a grudging style of assessment so consonant with manly reserve that he pretty much remained all boy. Still, it seemed to me only to be expected that, directly after these stupendous three words had borne out just how pretty and witty and gay Maria truly was, her fellow shop girls should accuse her of being also out of her mind.

Which what where whom · "I may still hear 'I Feel Pretty' any Saturday night in the heart of Greenwich Village, at Marie's Crisis, where as soon as the pianist strikes the opening chords, excitement spreads like a giggling fit among all the men in the room, whose too-bright eyes at once solicit and evade recognition of the former times when we never dreamt of singing this song or would only sing it in private; or of a more recent period when in the course of singing it, having found in our lover a willing partner, we would dance stark naked all through the apartment. And yet by the time the song proper begins, its performance has been delegated to one man in particular, some Mary fizzy, and funny, and fine enough to play Maria for all he is worth (in other words, as if she were Violetta). To his hysterical impersonation (in which he shows an ability that seems wholly at variance with his corpulent body or bald head), our hands will accord the sound that says love, but our voices stick to the contrapuntal disavowals of the chorus: *what mirror where?* The entire scene unfolds as though we were playing one of those childhood games at the end of which someone (who each of us used to fear would be him) is left standing, or holding a hot potato; or as though we were unwittingly providing anthropological evidence in support of that theory of the emergence of Greek tragedy which supposes that, from a primordially undifferentiated chorus, the first actor was successively detached, isolated, victimized, and sanctified; or as though—for what was child's play, what is Greek tragedy to us but this?—we were in the workshop phase of rehearsing a typical Broadway production number, where in the midst of, for example, a full staff of handsome waiters, there suddenly appears, resurges as 'from way back when,' a certain wonderful woman with whom, while the room sways, they exchange identical compliments—she says to them, 'you're looking swell'; then they say to her 'you're looking swell'—and who, as the projection of an introjection, is deemed to be 'back where she belongs.'

"*IF MY FRIENDS COULD SEE ME NOW*" · "In true Broadway fashion, this song of exuberant, overbearing triumph conjures up a state of being *all alone and friendless* that it never altogether conjures away. For what real amicability exists between me and the friends on whom, by calling them to witness—but not share in—my success, I can only be hoping to visit a plague of envy, which in the worst case will exact retribution for their contempt and in the best impel them to make it up to me before (returning the contempt on them) I desert the stumblebums for good in favor of the top-drawer first-rate chums I now attract? Or between me and the friends to whom, by proffering them all this see-through bravado (wherein it is understood that I have no better chance at retaining such chums than Charity herself, prompted to sing this song, not just at the outset of her upmarket date with Vittorio Vidal, but also after his humiliating rejection of her), I seek to attach my-self through their pity? One night at J.J.'s, having joined in this song, which was a favorite of mine, I was struck dumb by the sudden consciousness that the days when, as they say in musical comedy, 'my life was a song,' that is to say, miserable, had in this respect passed: if my friends could see me now, they would see . . . *I now had friends:* new ones whose presence in my life was at once desired and undoubtful enough to drain of its primacy, even of its necessity, their imaginary presentation to the old ones whom—strangely pos-sible deed, since the latter had never been fond of me—I was actu-ally in the course of dropping. I stopped singing, as bewildered as if I had suddenly forgotten the words, or they had gone into a foreign language I barely knew. Although it often enough happens that a man's desire is betrayed by impotence, at other times, still more horrible, his impotence provides an embarrassingly faithful somatic transcription of desire that has in truth relinquished the object with which his body remains inertly entwined. It was the latter fate that befell me that evening at J.J.'s, amid a multitude of witnesses, as a certain once strong significance all at once went dead in me. I with-drew from the crowd around the piano, feeling sheepish about the unanswerable cruelty of my gesture, as though, in bed with my boyfriend, and in the midst of the most passionate embraces, I had as good as blurted out, 'I don't love you anymore,' and almost sad enough to cry over the loss of an old, until that moment reliable pleasure.

All I can say is wow · "For others at J.J.'s, however, and even for myself in other places, the reorientation that was fatal to the old meaning of the song furnished the basis on which a new meaning was able to thrive. On the disco floor, for instance, where, by no means the only show tune to do so, this song enjoyed a second life, those so-called friends were now supposed to be staggered not by such pathetically self-canceling signs of worldly success as 'a bed-spread made of three kinds of fur,' but by the truly lavish and jubi-lant spectacle of Gay Liberation. Holy cow! there, in a kind of huge cavern (but a cavern that the play of laser lights had somehow dis-interred, opened up to the stars), was their old scorned acquain-tance dancing with someone named *Joe*, and waving his hands vic-toriously in the air; they'd never believe it, but all at once, with a last vestige of propriety having waited until it was soaking wet so that he might appear to have no choice in the matter, he took off his shirt! He did this as negligently as possible, crumpling into his hip pocket the garment that had been pressed crisp earlier in the eve-ning, but in his heart—the heart that, thanks to the accelerated disco beat, thanks, too, to the small inhalator from which he took periodic deep breaths (the only suggestion that he had ever been an allergy child), was beating as wildly as it did during his first en-

counter with this same Joe in Collingwood Playground—the gesture had as much drama as if he had laboriously exhumed himself, and were about to display to incredulous witnesses (foremost
among whom: himself) that resurrected flesh which, just as theol-
ogy had promised, was infinitely more glorious than that in which
he had been born. And if, as produced on the Broadway or the
basement stage, the song had only been able to intensify the solitude that it solaced, under the performance conditions at Dream-
land, its center of interest shifted from the absent old friends and
even from the also absent hoped-for new friends, to the friends
right there on the dance floor. Consonant with this new setting, the
lyrics were supplemented by the injunction, unthinkable in the de-
spairing, mean-spirited original, that 'I rejoice with all my friends.'
Surely the only *descamisados* that Evita could practically have had
in mind (when, following Charity's example, she sent her regards
from Broadway in the form of another show tune become disco
classic) were these handsome, mustachioed shock troops who made
war—our war—by their public way of making love. If I could see
them now.

"*SHALL WE DANCE?*" · "With his far-off way of singing a
favorite score, a certain chorister by the piano (X is all I yet can call
him) reminds me of Anna in one of her romantic trances: as when,
say, oblivious equally of her middle age, of Bangkok where she lives,
and of the King of Siam to whom she has been speaking, she begins to sing and dance in the character of a young English girl at her
first ball. Or in other words, excited by X's reverie, where lapped
in his music and his memories, he is not, nor ever could be, thinking of me, I remind myself of the King. My desire: that X forgo the

fantasy object in 'two black shoes and a white waistcoat' that sustains his remoteness and notice me here present, albeit in bare feet and the quite different finery of a red bolero jacket with gold brocade trim and matching breeches. But that I should be able to retrieve him from a rapture whose exclusive power was probably first entrenched in the solitude of childhood and is still fortified with the much denounced, but too seldom indulged pleasures of solipsism—this seems as little likely as that, in the politics of representation circa 1951, an Anglo-Saxon lady should be the new romance of a third-world polygamist. Or perchance, I more hopefully speculate, whenever a subject goes private in public thus, he is not so much disconnecting himself from social circuitry, as wiring into it the teasing and seductive effects belonging to a recessive self-image, all of which he may disown, but any of which, if he likes, he may also cultivate further. For if she *had* wanted to seduce the King, or even just to flirt with him, while at the same time eluding her Victorian superego, Anna could hardly have hit on a happier device than the absence of mind in which she unwittingly imparts to her fast-learning protégé some main conventions of Western courtship. And in the abrupt access of emotion that shakes and almost stifles her song after she comes to, she has surely met the King's ardent stare with a clear understanding of what was available as the meaning of her words, indeed of her whole performance, from the very start: *this kind of thing* can *happen.* Likewise, might not X, no longer self-exiled with his cast albums, but singing in the company of a whole expatriate community, be harboring an obscure wish that, of all those he lets witness his absorption, one would find it charming? Might not he even perhaps sense that he looks handsomer in this attitude than in any other, or, by a well-known law of erotic attrac-

tion, is more worth wanting? On such a basis, at any rate, I consider how, without the King's authority to command attention, or his right to bare his chest, I might embark on my new-formed project of getting the voice of a man whom I do not know well, or even by name, to break like Anna's, and for the same reason. With a compliment to his singing ('You dance pretty')? a question as to which show the song is from ('Teach teach teach')? I bet on the same dream-thick atmosphere through which introductions and invitations must lumber (and which sometimes leads me to despair of being able to cruise here), that later, when the last little star has left the sky, and the last patron the bar, it will prove to have begotten a dance with all the vulgar rustic briskness of Anna and the King polking on the palace floor.

"SOME PEOPLE" · "Like a window dresser who labors furiously on his mannequins, still readjusting a hem or the angle of a hat at the last minute before (the curtain being taken away) they must appear in careless glory, avatars of a style too accomplished to leave any trace of the toil needed for accomplishing it, so, some people supposed, M had secretly devoted every hour of free time to committing Broadway songbooks to memory, and to reviewing scores long forgotten, along with some that were at no point well known, all so that come Friday evening (the 'good night' at J. J.'s) he might amaze us not only by his exact and comprehensive command of 'the words' (to his distinct enunciation of which I was not alone in owing the sudden illumination of many a line previously only got

through mumbling and in confusion), but also by the unpedantic ease with which, whether identifying a song no one recognized, or performing an unknown verse from one familiar to everybody, he carried such great wealth of knowledge. One night, however, we heard him commit a blunder that even a newcomer to Friday nights would have found horrendous. We were singing 'Some People,' the part where Rose recalls for her father what 'Mr. Orpheum,' supposedly of the eponymous vaudeville circuit, has told her in a dream:

> 'Get yourself some new orchestrations
> New routines and red velvet curtains
> Get a feathered hat for the Baby
> Photographs in front of the theatre . . .'

But in place of the last line, M had substituted—thanks to his precise diction there was no mistaking his words—'Go to Schrafft's and run off the theatre.' No doubt the corruption dated back to his childhood, when he had first learned the song from the cast album, and if it threw every man of us at once into the heartless state of being embarrassed *for him,* the reason had less to do with its inaccuracy or apparent absurdity than with its sense. Too plainly did it betray his provincial juvenile desire, even more impatient than that of Rose herself (who at this point in the show is content with merely getting to L.A.), to dwell in some fanciful New York where people were always running off *to* the theatre—so the condensation was to be understood—and Schrafft's was the Stork Club by another name. With the silent cruelty of a maître d', I mentally put him in the Cub Room, at a table in 'Siberia,' before a grilled cheese sandwich and a side of cole slaw; others, less hypocritical, didn't hesitate to snort out similarly malicious asides. Yet when one came to think of it, his ridiculous error was really much worthier of our envy and admiration than all his otherwise impeccable knowledge. For it gave proof that M had truly *had a dream,* of sufficiently violent strength and urgency to overbear sense and even grammar—that, in the eagerness he shared with her *to get up and get out,* a small boy living life in a living room had gone so far as to outspeak outspoken Rose. More: the power, the aggression of imagination to which his clumsy nonsense testified was far closer to the source of Sondheim's elegant wit than was our sarcasm, which (though it had adopted some of the latter's surface postures) only revealed how frightened we were of our own originality, of the consequences of thinking, as each of us couldn't help often having occasion to do, *some people ain't me.* So the song to which M had botched the words, precisely because he had done so, belonged to him by an even better right than all those he had merely got perfect.

"EMPTY CHAIRS AT EMPTY TABLES" / "YOU COULD DRIVE A PERSON CRAZY" · "During one of my first times at J.J.'s, the pianist played a medley that, though I could hear the people around me sing it with as much fervor as if they were embarking on a crusade, I absolutely failed to recognize. The music wasn't merely unfamiliar; it had no more in common with the Broadway idiom I knew than a collection of religious hymns or pop ballads. And yet, strangely, it seemed able to inspire the same devotion, the same reverence on the faces of the men singing it (a few of whom seemed to be holding back tears) as *The Sound of Music* might have done. Even when, after a few subsequent visits, it was impossible

not to have learned these songs by rote, and to have also become sufficiently well acquainted with their source, I continued to exempt myself from singing them, sometimes by assuming the benign expression of one who is only pausing to catch his breath, at other times by vacating my seat on the pretext of a getting a drink, or using the toilet. Once, with R, I pretended to have a headache—or had one truly been brought on?—so that we could retreat to a table in the corner. But these embarrassed, almost bewildered withdrawals stemmed from a feeling that would have been more plainly expressed if I had all at once arisen from my stool in a grand fury and stormed my way to the door—jostling whatever furniture stood in my way, and leaving the clientele I had displaced from it to wonder at my departure, until one queen, more discerning than the rest, or perhaps in greater sympathy with my motive, should whisper confidentially: 'You *know* how she hates *Les Mis!*'

They could see a world reborn / A zombie's in my arms · "At the table in the corner, or elsewhere, R and I would launch into an insane debate, pointless since each of us secretly took the other's side as well as his own, whose topic was this same show: not its merit (which, since R's favorite musical was *Company,* directed by him in college, there were limits to how far he cared to defend) so much as the nature of the principle that lay behind my aversion to it. I would hold—for in this dispute I played the part of a student of aesthetics—that in any formal sense of the term, *Les Mis* was simply not a Broadway musical at all. Song here had nothing in common with the musical tradition established by Gershwin, Porter, Rodgers, Styne, Berlin, and Coleman, and continued even by Sondheim, and dance was lacking altogether. But worse than that, the sung-through character of the show destroyed, along with the fundamental structural opposition between narrative and number, those continual feats of negation that made the Broadway musical uniquely, preciously utopian. And another thing: whereas, in the show tune, this Neverland still expressed the misery that always survived so manifestly forced an attempt to deny it—an attempt, in any case, conspicuous for lasting no longer than the brief duration of a number—by contrast, the unbroken lugubriousness of the score of *Les Mis* (a show in which the few characters who don't die remain permanently guilt-tripped by those who do) conduced to so numb an acquiescence in the status quo that it was doubtful whether the same theatregoer who had just finished weeping for 'the miserable ones' even recognized them when they reappeared outside the theatre asking for spare change. On I would rave, working all the charms that my pedantry, my passion, my ironization of their blend could add to my argument, in the hope of convincing R, in the first instance, of those very charms (for I was on the verge of finding him everything a person could wish), and, in the second, of the fact that the secret—and only valid—object of that continuous threnody known as *Les Mis* was not Fantine, Gavroche, Eponine, Valjean, or any of the others, but the artistic form that it had taken over, like some zombie one could only shake in one's arms and scream at: 'But you're not the Broadway musical! What have you done with it?!'

Tomorrow never came / Not a person's bag · "R would hear me out, unconvinced, and then proceed, perhaps as befitted one who knew he was good in bed, to lay all my aesthetics on the couch. According to him, I was simply rationalizing the fact that during my childhood and adolescence, *Les Mis* did not yet exist. I therefore had no opportunity of confiding to it, in secret encounters with the cast album, the passions of which it would have been forever after the priceless repository. As the emotional richness of certain shows was simply the return on one's old psychic investments in them, it followed that without this opportunity, *Les Mis* would never be a true musical for me; it would always seem bloated with pretension, or silly with platitude; and I would sooner honor, in the spectacle of the men now singing it, the spray of spittle coming out of their mouths than the flow of tears that was engraving a senseless, ridiculous piety on their cheeks. But in fact, this grotesque spectacle was identical to the one in which, under another name (precisely, for instance, that of *The Sound of Music*) I was manifestly moved by my inclusion. Only now I was witnessing it from the outside, from a stranger's perspective, as though suddenly, at my mother's table, I had adopted the exigent criteria of a restaurant critic, and found fault with the cooking or the seasoning of what had been my favorite dish, the source of my captiousness being merely the fact that I was no longer partaking of a communion of love. (But he would say all this with a faint impatience, almost a mockery in his voice, as if the severe food reviewer were really himself and I the unsatisfactory meal that would never receive his indulgence.)

O my friends my friends forgive me / If he actually was dead · "My dislike for *Les Mis* only increased during the period when a song from the show, 'Empty Chairs at Empty Tables,' with its obvious appropriateness to the survivors, would be sung at memorial services. At R's, where its performance was intended to pay tribute to his well-known love of musical theatre, it had instead the effect of making me feel that, by an appalling coincidence, or thanks to those deep spiritual affinities that require old married couples to die within days of one another, the Broadway musical had passed away with this man who had loved it. Both now were being remembered in as distorted a fashion as if one had mistaken an ugly, pretentious tombstone for the perfectly proportioned body that was, for no good reason, decaying beneath it. Was it now only as an AIDS allegory of the most direct and immediate kind that the musical theatre could be meaningful in gay culture, or that the attachment to it could be justified? And who would ever bear witness that it was loved for other, older and deeper reasons if so many of those who could do so—and in R's case, do so in the simplest possible way, by the evidence of his own personality—would now, as the singer would eventually get around to telling us, *sing no more?* To myself, arid-eyed and incapable of any emotion deeper than this exasperation, itself deadening, it seemed that this song, by robbing me of my time-honored way of getting through difficult moments, had taken away the possibility of facing this one at all. Yet why should it? Remembering those old women in the churches of my childhood who would whisper their rosary in complete indifference to the mass in progress at the altar, I drifted into a less funereal service, from which Marius was banished, and his place taken by Marta, Kathy, and April, all somehow performed by myself (no less miraculously equipped with the vocal gifts to do so) as I brightly rendered a song from what at least *one* person in attendance knew was R's favorite show. It was particularly well suited to call him to mind, because, when we first met, he taught me a patch of it that had indeed been *harder than a matador coercin' a bull* to make out on the recording; and because later on, when he left me flat, I took a mad comfort in playing it repeatedly, which of course made me—gladly—want him even more.

"THE BEST OF TIMES IS NOW" • "I used to think this song perfectly illustrated the rhetorical double-dealing typical of show tunes, in that, though proclaiming the value of carpe diem, it encouraged only that of the deepest-dyed nostalgia. Between the old-times simplicity of the music and the lyrics' remembrance of forgotten yesterdays, the day that it pretended to urge us to seize could never dawn: there was no 'now,' or none that wasn't so empty an abstraction that it had to be willfully repeated ('is now, is now, is now') in the vain hope that formal reiteration could give it the content it lacked as anything except a synonym for 'then.' Whence the tears that this song, a regular crying machine, was so skillful at extorting from us at J.J.'s where it was extremely popular (the melody, too, being as friendly to our motley voices as the lyrics were to the faultiest memory). Yet precisely at J.J.'s, in the course of repeatedly singing it in the chorus there, I realized that I had altogether misunderstood the song, of which the truth (in these performances at any rate) lay not in the opposite of the literal meaning, but—just as this meaning held—in the joy of a present moment that was, in fact, amply substantiated, for it was none other than the moment of *singing the song.* This was a moment that you couldn't *not* make last so long as you sang it, and that would be truly worth regretting when you had lost it to the silence whose

Michael Perelman, *Stormy Weather*

properties here nowadays included the peculiar capacity to expand, like a poisonous gas, until it had touched everything about you with mortal stillness, including in no frivolous sense (so close is who we are to what we love) the dying, dead Broadway musical. So, better than any other, the song embodied for me that practice of the piano bar which let this obsolescent institution, out of fashion, out of date, speak to the situation of gay men at its most grimly 'topical,' and which consisted in holding fast to an experience of pleasure for which—with yesterday unforgotten, and as for tomorrow, well, who knows?—now is not the best of times.

Too far away · "When I saw the padlock on the doors to the place, then, my dismay could not have been more extravagant than if I had seen an angel with a flaming sword standing guard in front of them. Eventually, after an interim during which a notice pasted over these same doors promised us that J.J.'s would reopen shortly, and later, with no more truth, that it would be relocated at some date 'to be announced,' the very building it occupied was razed. I was never able to verify any of the gossip that spoke of evaded taxes, coke habits, and would-be original sins; perhaps it served less to explain the catastrophe than to console us for it by setting it on a grandly lurid stage replete with the most distinguished motifs of decadence the period had to offer, as though this small provincial bar, in which most of us never did anything worse than scratch the piano top with quarters to make tap sounds, had been Studio 54, or the Mine Shaft, or La Cage itself—any of which legends, however, caught precisely its allure for us as *the* place. At J.J.'s old site on upper Fillmore Street now stands an Italian clothing emporium— open, bright, spacious—called 'Cielo,' and when I pass by, if I am in a mood to make the best of the melancholy in which the sight of its young salesmen in azure jeans and billowing white shirts plunges me (or from which, rather, it reminds me that I have not emerged for quite a while) I tell myself, *joking but choking back tears,* that, like Joe in *Cabin in the Sky,* or Billy in *Carousel,* not to mention all those Cats, J.J.'s has passed into heaven.

Is now, is now, is now · "So imagine how overjoyed I was, years after J.J.'s closing, to rediscover the pianist, playing at another bar! I was thrilled too at the smile of recognition that, after so many years, he bestowed on me (though at no point did he ever know my name) as if I had been Dolly herself returning after a long absence, but looking swell as ever, to resume her rightful place in the Harmonia Gardens. But nothing was the same: the affectation of his world-weary air now consisted, I felt, in pretending it was affected. For to be weary, he had good cause. His new place of employment stood, alas, in more ways than one, at the bottom of Fourteenth Street, and his piano here was electronically amplified, homogenizing what could no longer be appreciated as the great smoothness of his playing style. Not that the latter wouldn't have been lost in any case on this crowd (in which I might have thought I recognized one or two familiar faces, if any of them had recognized me): so drunk, so beyond caring, that though everyone was wailing, as it seemed, at the top of his lungs, no one knew the words to anything, not to *La Cage,* not to *Mame,* not to *Gypsy!* But what most dejected me was the transformation of myself into the implacable person who was noticing all this, and who could notice nothing else. The words the others had forgotten, I was no longer able to pronounce. And if I had managed to utter them, I now doubted that these former Sesames should ever again give me access to that resilience so bravely contemptuous of the suffering it thus could dismiss. 'Finished? We're just beginning!' Instead, the brightest lines sounded in my mind (which could not obliterate them) like so many mocking dooms: *We never had the love that every child oughta get, A person could develop a cold, That's how young I feel.* —'Oh, honey, get over it!' But I had become—the very antitype of a character in musical theatre—someone who couldn't get over it. And in fact, though I left after a short while, throwing more money into the pianist's bowl than I ever had when I used to hear him regularly, I still occasionally return there or to other such places; just as when the finitude of human forms, or at least the finitude of the types by which I classify them, sometimes allows me to think that I recognize on the street someone who, as I remember almost at once, has been dead for a decade, I run ahead anyway to lay eyes on a likeness I know will never be quite exact."

On Broadway

Knock, knock • Recall how Linda Low, hearing a whistle on the beach, immediately turns around, happy to know the whistle is meant for her (whose enjoyment in being a girl must be considerably heightened by the relief of being rescued as one from the social and narrative nullity that would otherwise claim the young woman of her day); or how Lancelot du Lac, receiving Camelot's call in far-off France, has this instant recognition: "c'est moi." With the same peremptory familiarity did many of us who would become gay men feel addressed by the Broadway musical, which hailed us as directly as if it had been calling out our names, and met us so well that in finding ourselves called for, we seemed to find ourselves, period. But Linda and Lancelot are always cognizant that they are being called *to a calling,* to a social role (the Girl, the Hero) whose self-evident value runs everywhere through the national culture in which they perform as "persons of the drama." That the politicians of the New Frontier should have seen their own vaunting ambition in the Knights of the Table Round is as small a wonder as that, in "the home of a brave and free male" where her future lies, Linda's curled eyelashes will bat in time to the national anthem. But at no moment in his early cave worship of the Broadway musical—least of all when, whirling in tearful raptures before a squat totem of cast albums, he first extemporized the sacrament that infused into his awkward body unprecedented new grace—could the boy have enlightened us as to how such a deity had happened to command his attention, or to what ends it was leading his devotion. And while his secret subterranean ritual is brought to the light of day in the elaborate liturgy of the piano bar, where it is celebrated before a full congregation, in vestments of cashmere and silk, and with all its parts and gestures fixed, its officiant there, though now sure that, just like a close-binding mother or an absent father, *the Broadway musical made him homosexual,* is no more willing to elaborate this truth, which he possesses only in the short-circuited form of a joke, than the boy was able to discern it. In a word, this summons—inaudible except to the fine ears of the boy so justly called sensitive, but who, though he picked it up consistently, over several decades, and often in social regions quite remote from the Broadway beam, was nonetheless as deprived as everyone else of any means of knowing to what strange vocation, in hearing it, almost as if he had held in his hands *some divine divining rod,* he was being pointed—this summons calls for explanation.

Who's got the pain? Merle Louise (an early Baby June): "They used to say Merman never liked gays. But we went to this club once in Detroit, and it was a gay club—and everyone was surprised she went in the first place. One of the men asked her if she would please sing a song. And I thought, 'Oh, Jesus.' But she said, 'Sure.' They had this piano that wasn't in the greatest tune, and she sat on top of that piano and sang 'There's No Business Like Show Business.' And those guys wept. We all did" (Dennis McGovern and Deborah Grace Winer, *Sing Out, Louise!* New York: Macmillan, 1993, p. 155).

Regards to Broadway · Accordingly, to the vantage points from which we have so far observed the gay cult of the Broadway musical, the basement of its origins and the bar of its later institutionalization, we add a third: a seat in the theatre where its sacred texts—the musicals themselves—are performed. For it is only in the close engagement of an exegete with one of the latter that one may demonstrate, as a fact about its formal organization as basic as the division into acts, the presence and operation of that historically incontrovertible "gay subtext" which is never given literal expression, may never be acknowledged or even intended by those most immediately responsible for producing it, but which receives a kind of utterance nonetheless, as we will see, via a structural torsion of which the stress is sufficient to pop accepted themes out of their literal grooves onto another scene of signification, implicit but effective, where, for instance, Linda Low thrills men into wanting to *be* her, an identification that, for his part, young du Lac, whose prattle of his perfections yields nothing to Linda on the phone, seems already to have accomplished.

Touchstones and such stones as them · The stuff of mass culture (as our first culture) conducts psychic flows with an efficiency that the superior material of no second, later culture ever comes close to rivaling. It is by way of *Shane,* not Sophocles or Freud, that Oedipus stalks our dreams, just as the Beach Boys have a power of refreshing our memories unknown to Brahms. We do not begin to understand how fundamentally this stuff outfits our imagination of social space, and of our own (desired, represented, real) place in it, by refusing to acknowledge the stains that such flows may have deposited in a given sample. On the contrary, our cathexes correspond to an objective structure of soliciting, shaping, and storing them that contributes far more to the significance of a work of mass culture than the hackneyed aesthetic design, or the see-through ideological proposition, that is all that remains when they are overlooked. In any case, it is impossible to describe the appeal—let me insist: the *organized* appeal—made to gay men by the post-war Broadway musical as though one hadn't already heard it long ago. And conversely: if the example I now choose to document this appeal hadn't been the first stage musical I ever saw; or if I hadn't seen it in the sole company of my mother; or if these two exciting facts weren't set palpably reverberating against one another not only by a book that was about musicals and mothers both, but also through the amplification of an incomparably vociferous star: Merman, whom, from the distant promontory of a second balcony (in what my mother called "no man's land," her idiom expressing, at this Wednesday matinee, the more or less literal truth), we heard much better than we saw, but whose performance in this hazy perspective, though greatly anticipated, could never have disappointed me, never not have seemed larger than life—in short, if all these things hadn't forever after made me as little capable of finding a better example of the genre as a boy is of having more than one mother, then I would not now be in a state either of desire or ability to read the fortune that, on the road during the summer of 1961, this *Gypsy* first told me.

I

Some people can't even give it away · Now that all the tigresses have been driven from the theatre, their offspring may begin rehearsing for a children's talent show. The first child to perform steps forward: a small boy with a big accordion. A taunting fate has called him Arnold, the assonance of which hitches him far more securely to the bulky device sinking his shoulders than ever does the clumsy harness that suspends it from them. But even supposing that Arnold were not materially overwhelmed by his accordion, or just as hopelessly burdened by the spiritual impossibility (thanks to the implacable tigress who supervises his daily practice) of ever attaining the self-assurance required to play it well; even supposing he were to strut the thing with the cocklike brio of a junior Myron Floran, swelling the bellows more heartily than if they had been an extension of his own meager chest, and sneaking sufficient breath to pump them through teeth bared in the perfect likeness of a smile—even supposing all this, he wouldn't stand a chance against a simpering little girl completely covered with balloons, in whose favor the contest is being thrown by Uncle Jocko, its oily master of ceremonies. "Chip off her sister's block," the pseudo-Scot explains to his assistant, "and you ought to see *them* balloons!" Scarcely has he announced "Arnold and his Accordion," then, before he has the accordion overpowered by a sick chord from the pit, and Arnold by a stagehand who shoves him unceremoniously off stage.

When she has a smile, no one else has a prayer · Yet unless we delude ourselves into imagining that a fairer contest of this sort, decided by an honest judge or a whole panel of them, would ever award the palm to Arnold or his ilk over the Balloon Girl or hers, there is little point in bemoaning the venality of an emcee whose foremost crudeness consists in the attempt to rig an outcome so routine and even inevitable that it hardly requires intervention.

More pertinent is the general law of the musical theatre that Jocko's particular irregularity merely makes exceptionally explicit. This law ordains that, though male and female alike may and indeed must appear on the musical stage, they are not equally welcome there: the female performer will always enjoy the advantage of also being thought to *represent* this stage, as its sign, its celebrant, its essence, and its glory; while the male tends to be suffered on condition that, by the inferiority or subjection of his own talents, he assist the enhancement of hers. For this reason, though the balloons with which the girl bristles may be as vulgar, as comic in their way as the boy's accordion, yet they always hold a potential to lift her high above such terrestrial bodies as Drake, Raitt, or Preston into a milky way of stars like Merman, Martin, Channing, Lansbury, Andrews, Verdon, Stritch, LuPone, Peters; and even now, like the many breasts on a Hindu goddess, they radiate a divinity in whose penumbra Arnold's enormous instrument, no matter how stoutly he bears it, seems as droopy as a bouquet wilting in the arms of the stage-door Johnny who (one feels certain) will someday wait for her in vain.

Nice she ain't · Having, right off the bat, cited the law in question, *Gypsy* (of which of course I have just been paraphrasing the opening scene*) goes on to observe it with an unparalleled, one might say exaggerated stringency. With good reason did Kenneth Tynan lament "the lack, felt ever more urgently as the hours tick by,

---

*From the recently published version: *Gypsy: A Musical,* book by Arthur Laurents, music by Jule Styne, lyrics by Stephen Sondheim (New York: Theatre Communications Group, 1994). I use this text throughout.

of a good, solid male singer": not only do Momma Rose and her daughters engross all the narrative interest of the show, but, with a little help from some strippers in a burlesque house, they also command nearly every musical number. (Herbie's feeble solo was dropped during tryouts, leaving the only number remaining for a male principal, Tulsa's "All I Need is the Girl," looking even more extraneous.) And just as the other characters are domineered by Rose, so the other performers are throned over by the woman who plays her, a woman who (in the first instance) was famous for her ruthlessness in making sure that nothing and nobody on stage would ever eclipse her as what, even though she is no longer alive to carry on such efforts, she inarguably remains to this day: Broadway's greatest star. "When I do a show," Ethel Merman made no bones about saying, "the whole show revolves around *me*." She was affable enough to her leading man Jack Klugman, who offered even less resistance to her voice in their merely nominal duets than Herbie, whom he played, did to Rose's force of personality, but the young Paul Wallace, who played Tulsa, is said to have lived through the tryouts in dread that Merman would get his big song and dance cut. As it was, one evening in a nightclub after the show, the finest tigress in the jungle struck him across the face, saying: "You son-ofabitch, you're flashing your eyes when I do my lines."

Wherever I go, I know he goes · And just as *Gypsy* aligns its spectacle with that of the Woman more consistently than the star vehicles (such as *Mame* or *Funny Girl*) that follow in its wake, it also does so more "consciously": not only with a greater awareness of what it is doing, but (in an older sense of the word) a more furtive one, as though what it were doing partook in a guilty secret. The sign of both kinds of consciousness? that it always dramatizes this alignment differently, as also entailing a swerve away from men. Every female who enters the star spot is paired with a less brightly lit male figure, ridiculous or pathetic, of whom it is variously demonstrated that *he may not take her place there.* No sooner is Arnold sent packing, if he is lucky to earn his fortune in the Louisiana bayous with Queen Ida (and if not, to haunt the New York subways), than his place on stage is taken by a Dutch boy and girl called "Baby June and Company." Now the opposition between Arnold and the Balloon Girl, between the impossible performance and the inevitable one, takes the mitigated—and more familiar— form of a division of function within a single act, where the featured star is set against an anonymous collectivity that should swarm about her like bees in the service of the only fully developed female among them—that will so swarm, once this act becomes the production number that it aspires to be, and its present company of one swells to a full chorus of Newsboys and Farmboys, whose task is to dance attendance on Baby June until her big finish, when of course they must vacate the stage altogether. But now too the principle thus restated is given a twist that, in the American musical theatre circa *Gypsy,* is alone what allows Company's misery (unlike the twice hapless Arnold's) to be developed dramatically: he is not a boy. For lack of anything worse, Baby June's older sister Louise has been drafted into drag so that the usual show may go on.

That's how burlesque was born · In the topsy-turvy cosmos of musical theatre, the normal rights and prerogatives of the masculine role are beside the point to the girl here compelled to take it (and even to retain its sad costume, as emblematic as Cinderella's rags, when she isn't performing). What good are, say, all a boy's advantages at school if she doesn't go to school? Or the catcher's mitt she is stupidly encumbered with on her birthday when her world gives out status according to how well one plays the boards of a stage? And when this stage is an extension, a universalization of the body of her own Stage Mother, then she must forgo, along with the possibility of standing under the spotlight, that of being bathed there in the maternal love that pours down from it like a milk douche. As a boy, all that falls on Louise is the curse of young Marcel:

> LOUISE: June says you said she can sleep with you tonight.
> ROSE: You know how highstrung the Baby is after a performance.
> LOUISE: I performed.
> ROSE: It ain't the same.

Likewise, his so-called male entitlement dispossesses of everything worth having—of his mother, that is—the sissy boy for whom this boy sister is, to those with eyes shifty enough to see, a kind of rebus. (The same shifty eyes—heaven help them if they ever flashed!—would also observe that '50s psychiatry did not elaborate the figure of the "smother mother," any more than '50s sociology placed her on the horizon of "momism," to make us fear for her *female* children, whose dependency would have been if anything recommended in the period. Anomalous as the overbearing mother of girls, Rose owes her broad cultural resonance to the mass fantasy of the boys that, had she borne any, she would have impaired—not to say inspired—even more profoundly than the girls who thus make continual allusion to them.) But not being a sissy, being only the rebus of a sissy—a rebus, moreover, that, by the same open-secret logic responsible for proposing it, must be not merely left unsolved, but even abandoned as insoluble—Louise may do what the boy she "really" isn't cannot: she may dispel the pathos, and end the deprivation, of his state by a single gesture whose economy, in establishing her femininity and laying the basis of her stardom at one and the same time, already announces the elegance for which she will become famous. Whereas the boy wishing to be a star in this world must imagine himself in female dress, the girl may just take off her clothes.

Anything that's fresh'll earn you a big fat cigar · The sissified figure of the boy-who-would-be-queen, however, hardly disappears when Louise, reborn and regendered as Gypsy, ceases to embody it. On the contrary, in continued obedience to the logic of coupling every female star with a male star manqué, it rematerializes at the very moment of Gypsy's debut in the person of the stage manager of the Wichita burlesque house. No doubt the forbidden fantasy of male theatrical exhibition began gravitating for its trace-like expression (as joke, as slip, as what-is-sacrificed) toward Pastey, as he is christened, with the name of a basic item of striptease paraphernalia, from the moment the stage directions introduced him as a "young snot": for though a snot's hauteur may pay homage to the antitheatrical ideal of masculine reserve, his eagerness to play up that ideal, with every pose and pout of Attitude, manifestly delivers it over to feminine histrionics. Hence, even if it is the second sex that excites his desire, the snot will always seem to belong to the third: hence too, he inspires extreme rage in the men over whom he has any authority, since he makes them submit to what he also makes them recognize is the very incarnation of male submissiveness. True to type, Pastey, dubious himself, likes making others so as well:

PASTEY *(Snotty):* You Rose Louise?
HERBIE: Yeah, I'm Rose Louise.
PASTEY: Things're looking up. Well, I got a show to open, Rose Louise, so move your ass.

All too ostensibly mocking the desire for male performance, male femininity, male "ass" (each linked to the others in mutual implication), Pastey only flaunts his pleasure at putting it in play. Nor is the circulation of this desire exactly arrested with Herbie's uncharacteristically violent retort ("Listen, you little punk" is just his beginning), a bullying that, by publicly stripping Pastey of all claim to manhood, prepares the latter to *be* the abject figure for which he has pretended, perhaps in the hope of provoking his own exposure, to mistake Herbie. Thus, by the time that Pastey informs the burly theatre owner (bearing, after his prop, the name Cigar) that the star stripper has just been arrested, a certain pattern—tiny enough but visible to the shifty eye—is ready to reach completion. "Whatya want me to do?" Cigar retorts to him in exasperation, "Let you strip?" *Let?* Though it is Louise who gets the job, her performance is permanently marked by the implied rival who first announces it:

PASTEY: Miss—Gypsy—Rose—Lee!
TESSIE *(Correcting him angrily):* Louise!
(But he shrugs . . .)

So Pastey, whose slip here is telling, and even showing, forever defeminizes the queen of striptease: only nominally, of course, and only in secret (for everyone, ignorant of the name for which "Lee" has been substituted, will simply take the latter for a family name), but with an almost ritual emphasis nonetheless: as though his shrugging shoulders were sacerdotal hands laid on the woman who may now, with his blessing, hold the place not only of the boy she once was, but also of the boy he still is, the boy who otherwise couldn't help thinking that, but for her, the big fat cigar would be his. (And the point the librettist makes with this incident, the more poetical lyricist has already condensed into a couple of words. Just as by rechristening her, Pastey insinuates Louise's shady male past into her brilliant new career as all girl—or GRL, if we prefer the spelling on her monogram—so thanks to a rhyme whose imperfection our sense of its power to pick up the whole dramatic subtext of *Gypsy* would give him every right to shrug off, Sondheim conflates the self-assertion of her less famous colleague with the memory of a time when the latter had to bear, among other things, a masculine suffix: "Once I was a schlepper / Now I'm Miss Mazeppa.")

Pick up and pack out · Herbie is the only normal man to emerge in the world of *Gypsy*—to emerge from that world, rather, since it is precisely his dissatisfaction with it, and his dream of leaving it, for a house as private as private can be, that normalize him. And conversely: so long as he stays in the vicinity of the stage—for almost the length of the show—he stands, stoop-shouldered, as the figure of a masculinity disgraced by its subordination to an always more imposing femininity, in the same structural relation to Rose as Arnold does to the Balloon Girl, or Boy Louise does to

Baby June, or Pastey does to Gypsy Rose Lee. Though Rose, certainly, is not a star, or even a performer, but only, to borrow her
expression, "would've been" one, this narrative premise is instantly
and continually attenuated from the moment that Merman speaks
Rose's first words. And even if it weren't, the character who says,
"What I been holding down inside of me—if I ever let it out, there
wouldn't be signs big enough! There wouldn't be lights bright
enough!" does get her famous "Turn" to let it out on a stage, where
her performance even gains her some recognition (from Gypsy,
applauding in the wings: "You'd really have been something,
Mother"). Rose is far less manqué, in other words, than her ulcer-
ridden lover, who can only give his parallel declaration a pointedly
different turn. "If I ever let loose," says Herbie, "it'll end with me
picking up and walking"—and it does, with him walking not on
stage, but to wherever, remote from Rose, her family, her show
business, and her show, he may carry out the mission to whose
punishing terms he has at last acquiesced: "I'm going to be a man if
it kills me."

Everything's coming up roses · "You go to hell!" I hear one
of the deserted Newsboys shout after him, reiterating Momma
Rose's own parting curse. Equally flush with his Oedipal victory
and furious at Laius for never—so unlike Jocasta!—wanting possession of him, the boy has but one wish: to consign Herbie's duo-
denum to still fiercer flames. "Don't leave, Herbie, I need you,"
another boy, the one whose paper route Herbie would take over
when he was sick, cries out tearfully (also in imitation of Momma),
as though he were apprehensive that in taking at last the part of the
absent father to which his performance as the weak father had al-

ways been preparing him, Herbie might actually be going to his death. "Shut up and dance," a third boy (the eldest) urges on the others, attempting to recycle a consolation that—this too—Momma had once offered Herbie, and that consists in nothing but an even deeper investment in the musical that, from such deeps of despondency, has nothing to hit but the heights. —But no: the acoustic mirage fades, and I recall that, in fact, the Newsboys have "walked" even before Herbie does, urged by a necessity similar to his—there is no future in being Momma's boys—and, with Herbie gone, only her strangely hybridized Boy Louise remains with Momma on a stage whose lack of all clutter (the decks, the tracks have been cleared even of other characters) readies it for a finale which can be nobody's affair but their own.

II

You can sacrifice your sacro · Arnold, Boy Louise, Pastey: these mutilated figures, strewn by the way in *Gypsy*'s progress like so many atrocities on a warpath, bear the inevitable costs of a musical theatre that is divided by strife in fact. Of the two governments contending for rule over its spectacles, diplomatic recognition goes to the one whose leader Herbie calls "a prince named Ziegfeld." As is well known, this is a regime that promulgates a spectacle performed by Beautiful Girls and beheld by an Invisible Man whose desire (and whose power to have a theatre devoted to arousing it) they objectify. In other words, however, this is a regime in which the same man who enjoys the right to orient the spectacle also incurs the duty, if not quite to disappear from it (absolute renunciation being incompatible with plot), at any rate to forgo, in favor of secondary roles, that pride of place which he may freely take in almost every other sphere. And since the resultant tableau, though keeping him safely out of a woman's place (as the focal point of male desire), sets him at a no less distant remove from a man's (which is normally superior to hers), it remains able to scandalize the gender decorums that frame it. A man who did take the place of a woman could hardly be more abhorrent here than one who appears lacking in sufficient assertiveness to take it *from* her. It follows that whenever such a regime detects a man—and in particular a young man or boy—in the ambition or even mere wish to perform on the musical stage, it will be as brutal as is necessary to make a lesson of him: branding him with the repulsive character of Nerd, Sissy, or Snot, and maiming him so that he can hobble no further than the restricted mobility of these roles permits. If he must exhibit himself, the citizens' edification requires that he also exhibit his hideous scars—sores rather, as they never heal.

Momma is gonna see to it · Yet why should he brave such stigma at all if he hadn't been enlisted under the power—more ancient and tenacious—of a *solicitation?* For if he now finds himself putting up with a theatre whose clientele throws fruit at him, it is because his desire to perform was first exercised elsewhere, through a so much more heartening modeling of theatrical identities and relations that, in effect, he still hasn't left this earlier stage, where, just as he had taken his first steps, or uttered his first words there, he would sing and dance for a woman who called him to performance, and acclaimed him with applause even before he was through, prompting him if he faltered with some song or dance of her own, almost as though she were coaching him to be her understudy in a role that either generosity, or timidity, or some other thing kept her from playing herself. In short, contending against the established musical-theatrical regime that feminizes access to the performing space, a Mother Stage has universalized the desire to play there.

Momma's gotta let go · *Gypsy,* of course, presents a famously less rose-colored account of this Stage, which it only sights through the hostile optic of the jockos running a theatre of their own. Though the jockos never exactly win the war that is being waged at the heart of *Gypsy,* neither do they for a moment cease to command the value system underpinning the story. Laurents' book unremittingly draws Momma Rose in the cautionary terms of that "classic" psychopathology of murderous overprotectiveness, of endless self-sacrifice and ruthlessly exacted compensation for it, from which her children—and everyone else close to her—must sooner or later run for their lives. And beneath the psychiatrist's beard, as usual, an outraged patriarch hides his own, tacitly blaming Rose for leaving the house, or not returning to it when she has the chance; for bossing Jocko, Herbie, and every other man in her vicinity; for keeping that Babe June all to herself, and—worst of such emasculations—producing a boy like Louise, who anyone can tell will never be a man. Nor will this masked patriarch consent to forgive Rose, or discover a particle of unmonstrous humanity in her, until, abandoned utterly, she acknowledges the madness of dreaming that nothing was gonna stop her.

And if it wasn't for me, then where would you be, Miss Gypsy Rose Lee? · But while the jockos command the thematic perspective of the book, no one and nothing but the mother gener-

ates the performative pleasures of the musical. Book and musical
are not only distinct structural registers in *Gypsy,* but (contrary to
the received wisdom that sees here a masterpiece of their integration) so radically at odds that every positive value in the one becomes its exact negative in the other, and vice versa. "All mothers
out!": the very first words of the show (uttered by Uncle Jocko at
the Kiddie Show rehearsal) evince this ambivalence as directly as
"Who's there?" goes to *Hamlet*'s puzzled head. Take Jocko's order as
a thematic statement meant to initiate us into what the book wants
to say, and you must sooner or later assent to the desirability, if not
the practicality, of such banishment; but—equally inevitable—take
it as a formal function designed to frame what the musical is going to do, and you may only hear it announcing, by transparent,
but appetite-whetting antithesis, that jubilant *return* of the mother
which is the entrance of the star and the beginning (more to the
point than that of the play) of the show. And so throughout: Rose
may be a monster of a mother, but to her or her incitement are
owing nearly all the numbers, both "offstage" and "on," that make
this play the thing we want to see: a musical. And though June or
Herbie is doubtless giving proof of mental health in walking out on
Rose, they had better go to a therapist for validation, since the
spectator of *Gypsy* has withdrawn all interest from them at the moment it is clear that they will no longer be contributing to this
musical as such. The Good of *Gypsy*'s book can never sponsor or
even tolerate the songs and dances that are, after all, a musical's
definitive formal elements, but that find their sole rationale here in
an abnormality, a pathology that throws its taint on them. In this
sense, the supposed unsentimental diagnosis of the stage mother
only bespeaks the bad faith of the show, whose creators as well as

its spectators are no less dependent on this monstrous source of stimulation and pleasure than any Boy Louise could ever be. Should *Gypsy* ever be judged to deserve its self-allegorizing subtitle as "a musical fable"—or rather, since it has been so judged, could all that this judgment entails ever be spelled out—we would at last understand that the Broadway musical is the unique genre of mass culture to be elaborated in the name of the mother: a name, however, that it dare not quite speak—"m-m-momma m-m-momma" indeed—except now and then, on the well-known principle of any closet, to curse it.

And never gets carried away · This understanding would also enable us finally to recognize the theatrical function—beyond its dramatic context or its critical point—of Sondheim's irony. As everyone knows, his lyrics write into all the great formula songs of *Gypsy,* so insistently as to make it almost a condition of their getting sung, a morbid or sinister coefficient. Through its means, the first-act finale, in the course of rousing us to the requisite cheerfulness, enacts Rose's frenzy of egotism and rage; and other numbers, while celebrating as usual the couple or the team, betray the glib con jobs of this mother whose possessiveness makes the world so unbreathably small that, together wherever you go, you'll never get away from her. No longer can we entertain the optimism of the show tune without also linking it to a self-coarsening that lays a solid foundation for the eventual brutalization of others, or hear the loveliness of a love ballad and not hear too the hopeful bluffing and unromantic need casting out the line. Already, what will be recognized as Sondheim's characteristic method declares itself: he *psychologizes* show music, whether in the dramatic sense of tailoring

it to the expression of a particular—and particularly troubled—
character; or in the broader critical sense of demystifying whole
genres of Broadway song, whose unexceptionable manifest sentiments he marks with a deeper, darker complex of motive and affect
that has, it is implied, determined them all along. But *Gypsy*'s theatrical civil war allows us to turn the method on itself: to see all this
psychologizing (of which the resoluteness, as well as the brilliance,
lets it easily work a new enchantment in place of the old) against
the background of a psychodynamic that "places" it no less precisely
than *it* has placed a character or a musical genre. And this psychodynamic must strike us as necessarily more engaging than any
that can be discerned in those people-not-ourselves called characters, or offered to add to the bitter wisdom of those people-not-
ourselves called adults, since, unlike these, it is responsible for our
elemental enjoyment of the form itself, for those infantile, inti-

---

I wonder how old I am · There are ten candles on Louise's birthday cake, just
as there were ten last year and ten for untold years before that. Rose explains:
"As long as we have this act, no one is over twelve, and you all know it." The joke
would be a lot funnier here if the unripened physiques of the Newsboys—chorus
boys if ever there were—didn't convey the impression that her supposed impos-
ture can hardly be more than the simple truth. Albeit hailed as the great "book
musical," *Gypsy* is less bent on espousing the dramatic realism that would require
Newsboys who looked *too old* for their roles, than on elaborating the fantasy-
complex that is far more essential to its structure, and in which such choric
puerility may be simultaneously laid to the account of the *Mother,* whose wish to
maintain her sons' youth has actually arrested their growth; the *jockos,* who insist
that every male who takes the musical stage, however mature, be visibly marked
as no *man;* and the *Boy,* who willingly exhibits this brand in his eagerness to enjoy
the freedoms (of the Mother, of her stage) whose ignominious price it is.

mate, facile, fantastic pleasures which the musical numbers would procure us without benefit of such sophistication, and do procure us none the less under its cover. In other words, if Sondheim aims his irony at Rose, on this irony falls the shadow of another, larger one whose source is a mother, too: not the mother who is a character *in* the musical, and whom, quite understandably, we want to get once and for all out of our hair, but—and this explains the supreme importance of the character who holds her place—the mother who is a figure *of* the musical, and who, without problems, with nothing but our demand for her, anchors our primary pleasures in what is both the spectacle and the memory it recovers of performing in her vicinity, within range of her voice. (For, with, as her? *Gypsy* realizes all three possibilities.) The appetite for these pleasures may be disdained or disciplined, but it cannot be starved to death without affecting the livelihood of the diet doctor as well. Instead, Sondheim's so-called unsentimentality (which, rigorously pursued, would mean his abandonment of the Broadway musical) has the effect of one of those screens that modesty demanded accompany the public appearances of a noble lady in ancient Japan, or—smaller in scale—behind which Victorian gentility could safely commit the vulgarity of sucking on an orange at table: in mortifying our pleasures, in calling attention from them, it only puts an edge on our eventual "secret" indulgence.

I want your spirits to climb · Now, to such pleasures of *mothered performance,* whose shared, even blurred aspect does not allow it to be isolated on only one side of a proscenium, the logic of the musical number is deeply allied. For—when it works at any rate—this number is always destined to be, as we say, "infectious": to be caught and reproduced by the spectators who at a certain moment cease to be simply watching it (with all the distance, the evaluative superiority, that such watching implies), and begin, like the orchestra conductor who rises on tiptoe for a dramatic high note, or flings his arms out with a sudden expansion of sonority, *to imitate it*. At the theatre, this mimesis is both discreet, confined to humming the songs or tapping to the dances, and noncommittal, eliding the words and forgoing the dancers' actual postures. But for later, as everyone knows, we reserve something like a full-dress repetition! A brazenly public form, the Broadway musical secures its most important and widespread, its most cherished and enduring effects by being privatized, in a secret space of undisclosable fantasy where it becomes clear—or would, if anybody were there to watch—that not even the greatest performer has talent sufficient to keep us from identifying with her.

That's perfect for some people · Her. Hence, to a woman in the audience—such a woman, at any rate, as a man who can't forget how deeply he envies this happiness, or how bitterly he mourns his own forced renunciation of it, must imagine her—the Broadway musical is not just thrilling: it is *simply* thrilling. With no necessity of inhibition, or none at any rate coming from the social prescription of her gender, she may feel pretty, dance all night, enjoy being a girl. She may enter the heady fantasy of being the star of the show—of having been this star from as long ago as the moment when the show was first conceived as her "vehicle," and her many vassals got to work writing songs, sewing costumes, practicing dances, for their fair lady. And in this fantasy, when sooner or later she gets to assume that ecstatically martyred attitude, proper to mother, woman, and star alike, known as "giving her all," she will never have to face any difficulty as to whom, to which audience, she is giving it. For how should her imaginary performance ever be discomposed by the civil war that, in *Gypsy* for instance, catches a boy accordionist in the traumatic crossfire between a mother stage, where he was once encouraged to perform, and a jocko theatre, where his act is now censured as "what's gonna kill vaudeville" before being killed itself? That war hardly exists for the female performer, who on *Gypsy*'s showing moves from the early stage to the later one all the more inevitably in that, for her, either contains the other. Even at the start, only different niches in the same market separate the Baby's precocious splits from her rival's incipient balloons. And though Rose mindlessly grooms June for the jockos—in this respect, as Boy Louise is best placed to see, Momma is *not mother enough*—she is wrong to think she could ever really lose to them any girl of hers. Well before the curtain opens on Miss Gypsy Rose Lee in Minsky's Salute to the Garden of Eden, which her mischievous French tongue calls "le jardin de ma mère," the ecdysiast's debut in Wichita has already offered her occasion to regain the paradise lost to Boy Louise:

> *The only light on the stage is the glow of the mirror bulbs; the only figure is Louise. She looks at herself, goes close to the mirror to check her makeup, then suddenly stops. She touches her body lightly, moves back, straightens up, and stares at her reflection. Very softly—*
>
> LOUISE: Momma . . . I'm pretty . . . I'm a pretty girl,
> Momma.

It is perhaps the most moving, but surely the most invidious moment in *Gypsy*.

Smile, baby · The only thing that could possibly dilute such enjoyments is the very thing that renders them so pure. For a woman, they are as licit (that is, as banal) as those of sex in marriage. When it conjoins performance and femininity in the star, or when it implants this conjunction in the spectators' breasts—almost as though it were implanting breasts—the musical is training a woman in the same familiar affinities between herself and, say, spectacle (or say narcissism, masochism, her mother) that other mainstream forms of cultural representation have needed no catchy rhythms to be drumming into her all along. In receiving pleasure from the musical, not least at the delicious moment at which her ego-defenses surrender to being breached, overpowered, by the number's sympathetic hook, a woman becomes Woman, the cultural formula of her gender. That is also to say, her thrilling privilege recalls certain habitual obligations of her social performance as the second, subservient sex: those which it takes *a woman all powdered and pink* to meet, like the receptionist who daily replicates the star's glamour as part of her nothing job. So the utopia of female preeminence on the musical stage ends up bespeaking the reality of its opposite off that stage, in the musical theatre as well as nearly everywhere else. Pace Agnes de Mille, Dorothy Fields, or Betty Comden, a woman had better imagine being the star of the show; she could hardly become one of its creators.

Historical news is being made · The distinctiveness, then, of the Broadway musical in post-war mass culture is not that it leads a woman to inhabit the socially given idea of her gender—a project it shares, for instance, with fashion and cinema of the period—but that it seduces a man to inhabit the same idea. Stimulated by the mimetic mechanism of the number to the spectacular

pleasures of femininity, the male spectator finds himself placed in a
fantasy scenario whose inseparable, almost indistinguishable players
are mother and child—with the result that, of any man who hasn't
leapt for joy in the orbit of his Mame, his Mabel, his Mayoress;
hasn't picked a little at Marian; hasn't flounced at the gym with one
Maria and floated up the hills with another; hasn't taken calls as
Ella, Mella, or Mom, and called himself Madam, Mrs. Lovett, Miss
Adelaide, and Miss Lee; hasn't beat the flower drum with Mei Li,
while he bumped with Mazeppa or Melba and rolled merrily with
Mary past Meg, Molly, Melisande, Margo, and so many Maries that,
like Marta and her friends, he was nearly driven crazy!—it is safe
to say that he has simply never been exposed to the form. (To all
the many songs celebrating various aspects of femininity, there
are few male counterparts, and these few never manage to express
a truly opposite sex. The Seabee chorus of *South Pacific* may revel in
a hearty he-man horniness, but when it extols women's breasts—
as, emphatically, "the things they got"—its members thrust forward their own luscious bare pectorals.) Common sense thus
proves wrong in believing that, for men, the beautiful girls or
brassy dames that populate the Broadway musical stage have been
put there as a heterosexual incitement. It would be truer to suppose that they are put there as a conventional sign of such incitement, the better to advance the public relations of a form whose
unpublicizable work is to indulge men in the thrills of a femininity
become their own—whence, incidentally, the characteristic mask—
tired, bored, slightly pained—worn on the faces of most men in the
audience. For, as everyone recognizes, you can't get a man with
"You Can't Get a Man with a Gun." Notwithstanding the female
allurements to be seen on stage, even bold men get shy in the presence of the Broadway musical, in which, when they do not run

from it as fast as their legs can carry them, they go to great lengths to conceal, often from themselves, their interest and delight. On behalf of the lout who wears his aversion to the musical like the ribbon on a prize bull, it at least may be urged that he has grasped the implicit transvestism of the form, which, where men are concerned, isn't all that different from those old-fashioned college reviews which seemed to have little point but to put men—and to get other men to appraise them—in dresses. The same cannot be said for the lug, equally well known, who must prepare for the musical's pleasures by immersing himself in deep ignorance as to their nature; already in a state of abdication when he enters the theatre, he is taken in hand by the wife who bought the tickets and bears all responsibility for whatever happens while he reclines— drunk, asleep, at all events absent—on his seat. No doubt, in the privacy of the shower, say, either of these types may find himself surprised, ashamed or excited, to be washing that man right out of his hair. But only within that social formation famous for the fearfulness of the individuals comprising it, who have in fact much to fear, do we find large numbers of men brave enough to embrace these pleasures for what they are, the same men who, though careful always to park their car inside the markings, are sufficiently reckless to drive it to a bar where the cops take down the plate numbers.

III

Now my tailor's happy · On first hearing one of Sondheim's lyrics for "Small World," Styne famously complained: "Jesus Christ, Sinatra can never sing that song—no man can." He had a point, of course, and one that implicitly holds for almost all the other songs in *Gypsy* as well. For even when Sondheim's lyrics do not literally set *hair ribbons* to Styne's airs, or are retouched to take the feminine gender out of the first person, the songs are difficult—uniquely so in 1959—to detach completely from their original dramatic matrix, in which they not just are, but demand to be sung by women, and thanks to which a professional male singer would not be happier to vocalize, say, "I'm very versatile" than (the actual line to which Styne objected) "I'm a woman with children." Nonetheless, the same logic that caused Sinatra, just as Styne had feared, to pass on "Small World" (which ended up getting popularized by the voice, more maidenly than Frankie Boy's at its sweetest had ever been, of Johnny Mathis, who sang, in place of the impossible line, this presumably more passable one: "'cause I'd love to have children") also allowed him to record, from a score he otherwise neglected, a song that was eminently suited to a man and his music: "All I Need is the Girl," the only song in *Gypsy* that, in Styne's sense, a male performer *can* sing and in fact the only song that one *does*—the one whom Laurents beguilingly calls "the oldest, brightest, and best-looking boy in the act: Tulsa."

They can stay and rot · Tulsa! To this day, in any man who had once been a boy in a basement, the mere mention of your name suffices to revive the shiver of an antique admiration: as though this basement had been a prison (its small window being in fact darkened with a cage of bars), in which, not having your ingenuity or your daring, he listened to "All I Need is the Girl" with the same popeyed wonder he might have shown in announcing to the cellmate he never had: "Tulsa pulled it off! Tulsa got away!" Covered in the radiance of which he had dreamed with Arnold, or despaired with Boy Louise, you were his hero, even titularly (*gypsy:* "member of a Broadway chorus"), and he couldn't take his mind off you, or keep it from weaving into the Ur-text of *Gypsy*—the one by Laurents and Sondheim—a garland of legends about you, all based on the meager history of his own desire, but all as extravagant as the rhinestones that, given half a chance, Louise would have sewn onto the lapels of your blue satin tux. Yet with all the repetition, variation, and exaggeration that characterized them, his florid tributes also lodged an implicit complaint against you, whose fugitiveness he was always trying, and failing, to arrest by such means. Eventually, the legends grew dark and conflicted as (his history being further unfolded) he better understood the *fatum* that destined you, like your fellow heroes in classical myth, to leave someone behind—destined *him,* that is, the boy whose rhapsodies accompanied you on your well-marked way to the Girl, to remain dancing in chains and longing for the man that got away.

What game shall we play and when? · In one of these legends (still full of simple worship), they say that you appeared to him in the flesh, and under the name, of his college roommate; however unlikely the disguise (Vince having no interest whatsoever in musical theatre), he recollected you at once as the hero of his childhood. And then, no more than Boy Louise in the Akron hotel room (so festooned with underwear and overflowing with casually dormant carnalities that it might as well have been the so-called suite of this residence hall), could he take his eyes off the blanket in which you lay sleeping on two chairs pushed together, as if its landscape of mounds and ridges, of abrupt headlands and rolling hillocks, would allow him to surmise the secrets of your body as reliably as, for a geologist, a belt of volcanoes on the earth's crust would indicate the tectonics of the continental plates. But in fact, this landscape was so convulsed by seismic tremors every time you shifted position or drew a deep breath that no sooner had he identified a particular pinnacle than it would wander off, be leveled to nothing, or multiply into a range of half a dozen such.

Sure as a star · But in the Ur-text, too, your particular genius was to know how to elude the vigilance of those psychic sentries that ordinarily guard men from having to recognize their desire for one another. No doubt *Gypsy* forbids male performance in the same ineffectual fashion as a boarding school used to forbid masturbation: with a fullness, a loquacity of prohibition that establishes, shapes, and sharpens the very desire lying beneath it. But though failing miserably to *suppress* the desire that is thus, on the contrary, everywhere set up, the musical manages much better (aiming in reality at just this) to make it a *secret:* one kept, not unindulged, in closets as various as the sarcasm of Pastey; the rebus of Louise, Boy Sister; the mimetic fantasizing of male spectators; and even the obsessiveness of the prohibition itself. Wily Tulsa— truly the most intelligent, the most resourceful boy in the act!—on you alone it dawned how male performance might be detached from secrecy, shame, and secondariness, and you grasped this knowledge as you would have a talisman on a hazardous adventure. Thus armed, while your fellow Newsboys resigned themselves to dancing in its shadow, you stole into the sacred spot, reserved, as you were well aware, for the Girl, and secured against male trespass by Repulsion and Ridicule, those murderous creatures you subdued with nothing more than a song whose lyrics and melody are inferior to half the others in *Gypsy,* and a dance simple enough to cause any Cat, who had been put through infinitely more athletic paces for a mere callback, to caterwaul with resentment; and there, in that shimmering circle of light, though you were performing in a woman's vehicle to a jocko house that, God knows, was no home, there, Tulsa, you stopped the show!

Well, you see, I pretend · To achieve so much, all you needed was the pretense that all you needed was the Girl. It was a mere heterosexual formality, which you so well understood as such that, though you borrowed a lot from a 1935 Warren/Dubin song called "Lulu's Back in Town" (including its opening rhyme: "Got to get my old tuxedo pressed / Got to sew a button on my vest"), you didn't bring Lulu, or any other woman's name whose peculiar coquettish scent would have proved needlessly, even distractingly heady. The generic, hygienic Girl was all you really needed. But need her you did, whether or not you wanted her, understanding that the fulfillment of this formality was not merely a desideratum, but a necessity of male performance, which would never pass muster if it weren't a performance of, above all, this necessity. And while the formality might seem simple enough, here it required an intricate observance. However needful that you do so at once, it was not sufficient that you signify your heterosexuality *in general;* like a missionary who must adapt the expression of his religion to the language, customs, and beliefs of the natives he is seeking to convert, you also had to signify it within the particular context—the codes, traditions, self-representations—of *musical theatre.* Accordingly, you didn't just introduce your performance with this, as it were, theo-

logical postulate: "I'm home getting dressed for a date." You culti-
vated all during it acceptably male performance traditions, reviving
one such strain—the *debonair* dancing of Fred Astaire—by crossing
it with another, equally foreign to the Broadway stage in 1959—the
smooth and snappy vocalism of Frank Sinatra. And to these you understood that another sign, the most important of all, must be

→

For me, for me, for me, for me, for me, FOR ME · "Chance had introduced me
to an actor who had played Tulsa on Broadway (and played him so well that his
performance remains definitive for all who saw it); and I could hardly rest until
I had arranged an opportunity to ask him all about his great number, which I had
watched him do many times, and heard on the cast album many more. At first, I
experienced nothing but the most intense pleasure in the event, for, in order to
answer my questions (as precise as obsession could make them), this actor had to
withdraw into recollection, even to inhabit his old character again, and in his
absorption it seemed to me that the performance that had charmed me so greatly
was being extended, given an encore by my own request. But eventually this
same absorption of his posed a problem: it eliminated any possibility that he
would ever recognize, much less indulge, what I was beginning to understand
that my detailed, awkward, 'secret' attention to his past performance, or my
bookish questions and commentaries on it now, represented for me: a wish to
accompany it. And suddenly, in the vicinity of this affable man whom I hardly
knew, and from whom I had wanted nothing but the very conversation I was
having, suddenly I felt a degree of anguish, of agony, that up till then I had only
associated with my most desperate romantic reverses. —In short, I was under a
spell, one cast on me at the moment I pronounced, vis-à-vis someone who had
once happened to assume it, the all-too-potent name: 'Tulsa.' In that moment, my
body was shrunk to the puny stature, and reshaped with the ambiguous morphol-
ogy, of Boy Louise, and over it a huge figure—unaware of me, unaware of my
hopes—came to loom where an innocent middle-sized actor had just been standing. And the spell was never going to be broken until this hero, this cad, this giant
in the sky would crack his voice for me."

added, so as to accord your performance with the public relations of jocko theatre. Your performance had to proclaim, as its very motto, *the desirability of the renunciation of performance.* Without blinking, then, you affirmed that the same element that would give to your tie and your tweed their decisive coordination—that is, *the girl to go with 'em*—would also eventually demand that you willingly divest yourself of both items, replacing the unavowed eros of public performance with the authorized sexuality of the usual private show:

> And if she'll say, 'My
> Darling I'm yours' I'll throw away my
> Striped tie and my best pressed tweed.
> All I really need is the girl.

For you were confident that no one would see, or seeing, say he saw, that this virile warranty, which consists in a man's zeal to sacrifice his ambition, deemed worthless next to the love on whose altar he dresses it to kill, enunciates *mutatis mutandis* the same ideology inculcated in the Girl herself, on her way to becoming a housewife.

Little lamb · Not that in declaring this sentiment, you had any intention of honoring it. In your dandy sheep's threads, you were as hungry for stardom as the proverbial wolf, who to advance his ravenous designs dons a mask of modesty. "I don't mean I'm going to hog it," you told Boy Louise, "but—they always look at the girl . . . in a dance team. Especially if she's pretty." But if you were going to realize your "Dreams of Glory" (so placards on stage captioned your number), you would have to hog it, and they would have to be looking at you, at your fancy footwork, your fancier clothes, your own good looks. To this end, you were ready to treat the Girl to a deception worthy of Jason or Theseus; while feigning she was the star, you would in fact confine her to a token appearance—to appearing *as* a token, whose only function was to give an alibi to the spectator's absorption in you. But it never came to that (it was not the Girl whom you ended up betraying); for in fact, in the number you performed, more radical than the number you talked about performing, *she never appeared at all.* On your saying "All I need is the Girl," no girl was needed, except the one that—without the slightest censure—you thus got to become as you stepped up to her place before the mirror, that prettifying mirror of performance in which, no less than Maria already had done, Linda Low, Cassie, Christine Daaé, and Gypsy herself would stand transfixed by their star appeal, and proceeded to comb your hair, put a flower on, and show off a wardrobe that was a wow, even to the point of proclaiming, apropos of a certain step, that it was good for the costumes!

This step is good for the costumes · Things weren't much different in your later incarnation. A room in the basement of the dorm had been turned into a Discotheque, dressed out with papier mâché to simulate the cave in which people then liked to imagine that they were dancing, just as during the preceding dynasty of the Nightclub they had done beneath banana and palm trees. To inaugurate this new space, which had been your idea and your execution, at a certain moment on opening night, as you were standing in the midst of an appreciative crowd of men with their dates, neglecting your own, you suddenly dropped belly-down to the floor; onlookers might have feared the onset of an epileptic swoon, if they hadn't already recognized the initial position for a dance called "the Ga-tor," whose solo performance, to general delight and cries of "Go, Vince!" had just commenced. For two entire minutes, under the stalactites, the black lights, and the fixed eyes of everyone present, you jerked your limbs violently in imitation of the motion (or so we supposed, never having seen such a thing) of a large humping rep-tile, sending your body bouncing along the floor in spasms, until finally, when these could hardly become more frequent or furious, they subsided as abruptly as they had begun into all the humid in-ertness of a real alligator on the rocks of an aquarium—and you rose to smile acknowledgment of your applause, your white shirt-front soiled and half-undone.

Strings come in · If you succeeded in establishing your het-erosexuality without adducing a woman in proof of it, however, the chief reason was that you were all along corroborating it in a far more concrete—and crucial—way. For insofar as the Girl is an object of *need* (rather than *desire,* evidence for which was totally lacking in your case), heterosexuality describes not a spontaneous erotics, but a mandatory social identity; and as such, ever since the moment in the last century when the term itself emerged, by a kind of back-formation, as the "opposite" of another term that had just preceded it in existence, it has been constituted by this negative determination. In other words, what gives heterosexual identity its definition, its coherence, its prestige is the fact that it is *not homosex-ual.* It can sooner dispense with the Girl who is supposed to epito-mize its desires, objects, and practices, than with the Boy who in fact does epitomize the organizing obverse of them. So, your Girl might appear only briefly, or not appear at all, because you were also at the same time demonstrably rejecting that far less abstract being who was the Boy on stage actually watching you. For to state the obvious, unnoticed fact, it was precisely *as a boy*—dressed and otherwise socialized like one, even to the point of having "no talent" for performance—that Louise passed unseen in your search for a partner in the act. (Those literal-minded enough to remonstrate that Louise was not a boy are not literal-minded enough to remember that she bore the name "Plug," by which boyish entitlement you, Herbie, and even her own grandfather often addressed her.)

They take bows and you're battin' zero · But did you really not see? In later life Gypsy, almost demented by the passion she brought to the question, was obsessed with determining of what stuffs, in what proportions, you had woven the ensorcelled cloak that, cast over his shoulders like a mantle of deltoid muscle, made the Boy's desire invisible to you—of how much simple ignorance and how much active unknowing and how much sheer mendacity? But, as she might have known, you hadn't woven the cloak at all; cut from a bolt of the social fabric, it was a garment in common use that all men would throw over themselves and each other so that, in obedience to the cruel precepts of masculinity, such desire, like a caliph wandering his capital late at night and in disguise, would always be able to circulate beyond social or psychic recognition. In your own presence, Boy Louise had resorted to such a disguise himself:

TULSA: What do you make up dreams about, Louise?
LOUISE: . . . People.

Whatever you knew, saw, felt about his dreams, you also understood that your security depended on not showing any of it, on displaying instead, as conspicuously as possible, the insignia of a myopia that, had it been real, or extended beyond this one subject, would have ended your dancing career. Debonair Tulsa, how maladroit you became with the Boy, grasping the air instead of the hand he stretched out to you, lifting a phantom while a few yards away he prepared himself to be raised. But the spectacle of this failed, this unimaginable coordination was as essential to your triumph on the stage of *Gypsy* as it was to his misery in wanting to share that stage with you. You must always be seen to have no more reason to know that he was in love with you, than to suspect that he had been watching you from up in the flies every time you rehearsed, wishing it were he, and not a broom, swept into your arms, or that once, taking advantage of a time when no one was in the suite, he fished a shirt from your dirty clothes, the one in which you had done the Gator, and put it on, not to attempt that dance, but to touch himself pretending he was touching you.

Now the tempo changes · The same diabolically organized world that made a secret of the homoeroticism that it nonetheless never ceased producing, circulating, or exploiting also compelled every male who became conscious of the secret to guard it in a perpetual trust that there was, alas, no shirking. Let someone just try breaking the silence with an acknowledgment; when he did, others would hear only the wishful thinking of an individual, of a deviant whose manifestly tortured mental state they would never imagine linking to the contradictions of the cultural apparatus that was thus putting the screws to him. Either he must keep the secret to himself, or, perforce, he would be made to keep it *as himself,* identical and confined to the contours of a "homosexual" psychopathology. Dimly understanding all this, Boy Louise, whom underneath his adoring attitude vengeful Furies were urging to disrupt the show of your insouciance at all costs, rightly feared that if he did so, he should have to pay such costs entirely out of his own pocket, by making an unwelcome spectacle of himself. But he was mistaken. For when, as recklessly as if he were planting a passionate kiss on your lips, he all at once thrust himself into your act and began to do a step alongside you—this awkward gesture being intended, under the guise of a pathetic declaration of his desire, as a more provocative demonstration of your own—a miracle happened. "That's *it,* Louise," you cried, and as unsubornable witness to the excitement to which you thus surrendered, your voice suddenly cracked—rose up into the long superseded pitch of a girlish shriek. Through that crack, out you clambered, once again a boy (the "girl" in the man), come to take another boy (another "girl") for your partner. "But do it over here! Give me your hand! Faster! Again! Do it again! Turn!" Though the tempo had just quickened, it was equaled by the speed with which, given this permission, he learned to follow your lead all the way to the finale, when the odd couple uncannily precipitated from your right-thinking dream of a dance team ended, Laurents says, "together—in triumph."

All the lights come up · Later variant: you and he were riding the night train back to New Haven when, without warning or even preamble, he blurted out in the dark: "Vince, I have feelings for you." But instead of breaking into the laughter that the inane phrase, not to mention the manic abruptness with which it was pronounced, perhaps invited, and instead of going cold, or getting warm, with disapproval of the sentiments it expressed, you took his hand, and solemnly replied: "I have them for you too." And suddenly, decisively, all the lights came up! Only a moment before, he had been still shyly speculating as to what forms could ever express these feelings of his, forms that seemed to lie hidden, unspecified and indeterminate, in a turbid atmosphere that might take him even longer to penetrate than it had already taken him to recognize, as being somehow "physical," the feelings themselves; now, but an instant later, he found his mind opening a trove of gay pornography that it never knew it possessed, in which various models obligingly inventoried the main practices under an illumination that, while anything but harsh, exposed and clarified everything. Thanks to that single phrase—"I have them for you too"—his imagination ran away with him so far that, in what seemed like no time, the person who had got on board the train with you in Grand Central Station, the dimwit who just "wondered," would never be seen or heard from again.

That's it, Louise · When, soon afterward, you clarified your meaning—that is, denied it—by eloping with June (for you had begun to be persuaded of the suspicions, including some arising from within your own heart, that would eventually fall on a merely *alleged* heterosexuality), we suffered twice over. One grief, of course, was your desertion of Boy Louise, which had come without warning or explanation, as if so ordinary, so expected an outcome could require none. With this normality, no doubt, June had brought you an amnesia that put its prehistory beyond recall; whenever necessary the two of you now stoked the conjugal bed by retelling a narrative in which Louise had misconstrued your overworked vocal cords, inflated your feelings of simple friendship, made up the whole fantastic thing in his head! In appeasement of our resentment, though, *Gypsy* punished you for your treachery, punished you with all the satisfying fitness of a Dantesque contrappasso. Just when you dropped Louise in the story, you were yourself dropped from the show. You might break faith with the Boy, but you were held to the pact you signed with the Girl: she had appeared; she had said, "My darling, I'm yours," and now, before the end of the first act, you must return your costume to wardrobe. What did we care, then, that you didn't take us along?—you were going no place! and soon enough, you'd be calling some mediocre management job "challenging"! But our other grief was less tractable, for it was . . . this very punishment. You, who were supposed to be the great exception, now proved the rule; with your exile, *Gypsy*'s allegory of male performance achieved its most emphatic statement. We surveyed our depressed prospects: if we took on a man's normal social identity (assuming we could), then, like you, we would have to leave the musical stage; and if we chose to remain, it would be only as Newsboys, for we could never be so fully identified with a Woman as to get her starring roles. (The biology that was insufficient to establish us as real men remained more than enough to prevent us from assuming the prerogatives of real women.) Like a mother who both loves and loves dominating her children—indeed, in the figure of Rose, by means of such a mother—*Gypsy* held, but never surrendered a place for us, her sons. No wonder we were devoted to this show; no wonder our devotion, if it were to bear up under the contradiction bearing down on it, had to be nothing short of blind.

It's what grownups call a real romance · As to whether you and Boy Louise ever met later in life, after he became Gypsy, the apocrypha are more willing to gratify our curiosity than the

Ur-text that raises it. In one account, they say that after many years, Gypsy, who was playing in the town where you lived, arranged to meet you for a drink. She recognized you, of course, not noticeably altered for the worse, as soon as you entered the rendezvous where, as if for further developments, she was nervously waiting. But even after she had completed the physical appraisal—for all its rapidity, total and minute—that was her habitual first response to men (but which, the habit being of recent origin, you were receiving for the first time), she couldn't discern what she used to see in you. Except for your eyes, large open windows through which she still had the illusion of being able to see a vast Oklahoma sky, you were no longer a man who held the slightest embodied appeal for her. For half a decade, not a day went by, *not a single day,* that she hadn't prayed for this indifference (every prayer lapsing into a forlorn apostrophe to you instead of God, imploring to know where you were, what you were doing, if you ever thought of her), but now that it seemed to be granted her, she found herself confused, upset, almost on the brink of panic. She looked around her for help: but this old downtown "cocktail lounge," long deserted by the fashionable and almost empty, on this afternoon, of anyone else, nonetheless failed to emanate the melancholy bygone charm she sought—as though in taking elsewhere, not just their business, but the custom of their passions too, its clientele had walked off with the fixtures, with everything precious or even distinctive about the place, leaving it, rather than heart-breaking, simply blank. It was intolerable to think that you, still the agent of the worst crisis, the most profound modification of her life, were thus generic—that you might have been some other man, perhaps even (had she during her boyhood happened to share a room with him) any other.

Gradually, she calmed herself by withdrawing her attention from everything except your eyes, and she was more thankful than not for the apparent regression in you too when, by way of good-bye, you said in a confidential undertone, "You know, Plug, I've always felt about you——" then broke off, shrugged, and left her hooked and dangling once again.

Some old and then some new tricks · But in another version of this meeting, they say that Gypsy, far from seeking to reanimate past feelings, only proposed it to show you she had much better things to do in her present identity. Accordingly, she arrived at the rendezvous attired in a Lacoste shirt and jeans so tight-fitting that they defied you not to acknowledge the spectacular career she was making, as this or that number required, of taking them off nightly. Solicited thus, you ceded your mite of congratulation, resorting to the formulas that were now available for such occasions, but in doing so, as though refusing a blackmail by paying it in counterfeit bills, or as though fearing, even at this date, lest she misunderstand, you added something dry and almost hostile to your tone that kept these formulas (at least for one who knew it as well as she did) from working any affirmation. Let her have, for instance, your brief little compliment on her "bravery"; but she must take along with it your embarrassment, your disgust for anyone with her cause to exercise that virtue. In the same spirit, having allowed as how she would probably find your family life "all very boring," you proceeded to indulge the subject, for the remainder of the conversation, as fully as if you had believed the exact opposite. She never spoke to you again—unless one counts a performance in which she did a strip to "All I Need is the Girl."

IV

This people's got it · At all events, this much is sure: if Tulsa stopped the show, that was all he did: for when the show went on again (as in this business it must do) the principle whose continuous operation he had momentarily interrupted resumed its governing hold as well. We might have hoped to the contrary, but deep down inside we knew that the boy from Oklahoma—alas, like all the talents who played him—would never go on to bigger things. As early as her opening number, wasn't it already clear as the pealing of a brass bell to whom the star turn would belong? For if "Some people can get a thrill / From knitting sweaters and sitting still," our own sublimity came from hearing, coincident with these words, the first distinctive crashes of a prodigious storm that no mere man could ever be singing up, but only that legendary thunderer whose virility lapsed below the waist, even nominally, into the tail of a fish. Merman! We let the name resonate in our minds (as, thanks to its final nasal, it had often done in our mouths) like a tridentate tuning fork, or one of those high C's she was famous for holding. Her voice had been so long and richly plenished by musical theatre's best composers—with "Rhythm" from Gershwin, "A Kick Out of You" from Porter, and "The Sun in the Morning" from Berlin, was there anything it hadn't "got" or wouldn't "get"?—that in hearing it, we thought we were listening to the voice of Broadway itself. And as it shortly proved by sending up an effortless "Goodbye / To blueberry pie," this same voice, though it had blown like Gabriel for longer than one remembered, was still ridin' high. Neither the reports nor the recordings had lied: they said it was wonderful; it was wonderful as they said.

And this people's spreading it around · But in the same
breath, we were also being served notice that it was not with a Girl
that the latent song-and-dance man in us would ever be manifest on
the Broadway stage; it was—and only could be—as this Woman.
Here was no Rose, born to blush unseen, but the Star that Rose
vainly wanted to be. So well, for instance, did her inimitably tim-
bred voice preserve the memory of its glorious past performances,
giving to every word it intoned the density of a concordance entry,
that it had scarcely sung three syllables before "Some People" was
overwhelmed in thrilling recollections of "no people but show people." And just as her singing thus annexed Sondheim's lyrics, with
all the angry disappointment and desperation he sought to convey
in them, to the anthem of her own buoyantly ongoing triumph, in
the same way her acting instinctively brushed off the dark shadings
of Laurents' characterization (which could only come into their
own with the legendless Tyne Daly a quarter of a century later) as
if they were so much grime that, due allowance made for touches
of the picturesque, should not be allowed to spoil the appearance of
a famous monument. (Similarly, whenever she planted herself into
position for a number, she took care that there should be but a
single possible view of this monument: the full front one.) Under
the circumstances, our narcissism, having just withdrawn its investments from a high-risk security called Arnold, could hardly have
remained so imprudent a financier as to transfer them undimin-
ished to a little-known speculation named Tulsa (whom hence perhaps we defrauded as much as he did us, and earlier, too). It must
place them—now, at once, even before she invited us in the next
number to "pool our resources"—with this Star whose already unmatched incandescence, it figured, could only intensify from our
willingness to remain in her shadow and (for so sacrosanct was our

desire to perform that, of this strongbox in which we had deposited it for safe keeping, we naturally made a tabernacle) could only expand along the banks of votive candles we would gratefully illuminate before her icon at countless shrines offstage.

Here she is, boys! · If few musicals do not implicate male spectators in just so enthralled a relation to the female star, none names this relation in its own fable as bluntly as *Gypsy*. Here, with unique lucidity, we are allowed to recognize how all our need and veneration must transform the star, no matter what role she plays, into the familiar figure that every woman becomes once we bury thus our desperate, adoring faces in her skirts. Call her Dolly, Mame, Eva, or the Spider Woman; even call her Lola, Peter Pan, or Annie; by any other name, she is still a Rose, a Momma who returns each of us to the dependent condition of a Momma's boy fearful she will leave him, and take with her all his pleasure and even his continued vitality. I once knew a mother who, as soon as she witnessed her child's fits of breathlessness, immediately began to double her own inhalations, confident that her thus enlarged bronchial tubes could meet the needs of her suffocating son. To any man whom the musical has at once encouraged and forbidden to want her place—to any man, in short, drawn to the form at all— the Star must seem to be such a mother, and he the allergy-ridden son who, without a single proof of its efficacy, trusts in the former's insane self-belief. (The festivities at Rock Hudson's Christmas party were in full swing when, with Jerry Herman at the piano, Florence Lacey began an impromptu rendition of "Can't Help Lovin' That Man"; but then, her accompanist recalls, two hundred men "stopped breathing.") For while the Star is unthinkable apart from the Boy cloned in the phalanges behind her on stage or before her in the front orchestra, yet this Madonna of the Great White Way presupposes less a joyful nativity scene, where, for all his swaddling clothes, a boy is entitled and even expected to be a lusty cry-baby, than an anguished *pietà,* in which the same son is, if not crucified, at all events asphyxiated, deprived of voice and breath, and she alone has the right to wail. The strange fact, then, that we never seem to resent this right (which, on the contrary, we are ecstatic whenever the Star Mother exercises) depends precisely on the symbiotic nature of the fantasy linking us to her, and thanks to which her performance always comes to us inscribed, in the words of Merman's first-act finale in *Gypsy,* with the life-saving dedication: "for me and for you."

For me and for you · For instance (from that same first-act finale):

> You can do it
> All you need is a hand
> We can do it
> Momma is gonna see to it.

If, at its usual volume, the Mermanian vibrato echoes with all the hubbub of popular theatre—that noisy medium to which it represents, on the part of a species that must make itself heard over a scene change or call a restless house to order, a quasi-Darwinian adaptation—here, pulsating with unwonted softness, it escorts us into the quivering intimacy of a tête-à-tête, as between a child who has come crying to his mother and a mother who, by force of sympathy, starts to cry herself. It suggests that Rose knows the same panicking self-doubt against which, as soon as she recovers the terrible majesty of a Momma who will see to it, she erects herself into the bulwark of Boy Louise's defense. Far from portraying a monster, Merman's tremulous, all but tearful rendering of these lines convinces us that within her imperturbably, her stupidly bright determination, Rose has been sheltering as much tender affection for Louise as her despised alter ego, that housewife content with knitting sweaters, no doubt conveyed to her own son by means of those very garments—garish misshapen things which, though they hung on him like the patched rags of a scarecrow, must nonetheless have still warmed him with the same snugness that he used to feel when she would tuck him under the covers. (And doesn't Rose knit such sweaters herself, in having her children's coats made out of blankets?)

Momma's all alone, Momma doesn't care · But suppose the Star Mother no longer consented to sustain our belief that she sings for two? This, precisely, is the extraordinary premise of "Rose's Turn," *Gypsy*'s great, repugnant finale. How aptly Merman pronounced it "a goddamn aria," for (let some people opine to the contrary) the "Turn" deserves nothing so much as to be cursed. The magic it works is a black one, and potent enough to disenchant our relation not only to the Star Mother, but also, in consequence, to the entire form in which she allows us to believe that, through sharing hers, we have a place. No doubt the euphoria that normally characterizes this relation depends, not so secretly, on the dread that the Star Mother, before she calms and even reverses it, must also have excited: that of being exiled from her presence. Even under the servile raptures of the waiters hailing Dolly, anyone may hear the uncontrollable sniffling of the child who begs its mother to "promise she'll never go away again." But the screw of the "Turn" is not that the Star Mother breaks this promise—in fact, of course, she continues to command the stage as she has done from the start of the show—but that now, in the course of gettin' hot and lettin' go, she *refuses to be Momma*. The delicious milk of her patronage turns to sourness as the benevolent queen who had once urged us to "sing out" now informs us, in the changed character of a spiteful crone, that we lack talent altogether: "Talent for the deaf dumb and blind, maybe, but not what I call talent. Not an ounce of it." And in case we are inclined to miss the point (as of course we are, we would give anything to miss it), this hag proceeds to abridge the queen's device to, merely, "for me": which she repeats more times than King Lear declaiming "never" over Cordelia's corpse—and indeed, with a rage all the greater than his in that Louise is still here: the Star Mother's volcanic expenditure now signifies all the nurture she shall *withhold* from her child, and hence her murderous willingness to reduce the latter to the breathless state that Lear thinks only of protesting. "For me, for me, for me, for me, for me, *for me*": with this almost intolerable rejection of maternity, the Star Mother divests herself of her supreme symbolic function, the one that ensures the formation of the necessary "good rapport" between performer and spectator not only in *Gypsy* but in the entire genre of which *Gypsy* is the fable. Though that function is all she takes off, therefore, its removal is sufficient to render her "Turn" more obscene than the rawest bump-and-grind routine, an act not to be performed on this or any other musical stage. But it is performed, and from what had been our earthly paradise, we are turned away.

Momma's gonna show it to ya! · No doubt, we were getting hints of this peripety—this turn—from the beginning. If, for instance, the first outburst of Merman's vocalism had summoned the very hair on our arm to stiff attention, this wasn't simply because, more positively than any mere visual impression, it identified the greatest Broadway celebrity of all in propria persona. Less delightfully, it had also recalled other fulminations, storms that like the domestic or scholastic theatres they overclouded were altogether unmusical, and in which the thunder would roll out of the darkness of a mother's displeasure, and the bolts descend in the form of a teacher's yardstick. Thanks to this acoustic palimpsest, even as the Star was singing, a Fury raged at us for passing candy in class or having broken her favorite figurine. And once we caught the title pun of the first-act finale—even if Louise *were* great, everything would still come up Rose's—we could hardly ignore the fact that this Star played with loaded dice whose every casting won her not just a "part," but the whole show. Yet as we trusted that all her bullying would be for our good, and not just for hers ("I thought you did it for me, Momma"), such hints no more mitigate the eventual shock of the "Turn" than the various clues he has been sifting through prepare the reader of a well-crafted detective story against his amazement when the murderer stands revealed before him— even less, in fact, since, unlike that reader, we have lacked both inclination and incentive to foresee any such unforeseen discovery. Without warning, then, or with none that we were able to heed, we now face the awful possibility that "Sing out!" has never meant anything but "Shut up!" and, worse, that we have dimly understood this all along: it was the reason we could hardly raise our voices in the first place, why no real talent had emerged, or could survive in the Star Mother's vicinity. Even the hostilities of the civil war seemed less stifling to us than does the double bind that is suddenly shown to emanate from our leader in them: this con artist, as it turns out, who has rallied us to a place that only she shall occupy; who having modeled our performing desire stands in its way, herself the sole fit agent of its accomplishment. "Rose's Turn" may be the Star Mother's lesson in show-stopping, but all she means us to learn from it is that no one can—or if anyone can, no one may— sing out so well as she. "You like it?" she taunts her "boys," with the sadism of a child who, unlike you, still holds an ice cream cone in her hands, or of a writer who wields a pen more mightily than you can even dream of doing, "Well, I got it."

All your life and what does it get you? · Consider the disgrace of a lover so eager to have his passion recognized, or so grateful for its return, that he has tattooed himself with the name of his beloved; never dreaming, perhaps never caring that this inscription disfigures him until, jilted one day, he notices on his skin, where charming floriations used to be, the outlines of a hideous brand: liver-ripping testimony that he has made the most wretched of all sacrifices, an unaccepted one. And he has every reason to fear that his pain, sharper than the tattooist's needles ever were, will also prove so steady that they may as well have engrained in his flesh, together with the imitation rose, real thorns. For as long as he is thus marked for one alone, so long must he be repellent to any other; he will go on not just remembering, but reenacting the drama of his rejection to the end of his days! This only could make him more furious and forlorn: if every time a mirror showed him the bower in which, just over his heart, the name of his heartbreaker lay ensconced, he had to read the word "Mom." —It is to no less extreme a scarification, though, that we suddenly recognize having submitted body and soul. We had imagined that only the Star Mother could love us, and so gave ourselves the identity of creatures who could love only her: fatuous single-minded Friends of the Diva who ignored—suppressed—their own peculiarities the better to take the imprint, with a little lamb's docility, of every one of hers. Now she turns from us at the moment of her greatest triumph, and to this injury adds the insulting claim that all our sacrifice was really hers: she was the one who suffered the lack of recognition, and if we think otherwise, it only shows how selfish we continue to be. Now too, therefore, we understand that we would-be wise investors were never anything but a bunch of desperate gamblers, who having bet our whole stake on a losing game, must sooner or later reach this deserted point of—in every sense—no return. Pity this altogether artificial "Rose"? After all we've given her? after all we can't but go on giving her? We're no boy scouts; we could strangle her!

So much in common it's a phenomenon · Instead, our hands reach out only to strike one another; their short, sharp slaps, akin to a string of firecrackers set off in celebration of a national holiday, denote nothing more sinister than the sound of an ovation, the ovation that, after all, we never fail to accord a perfomance of "Rose's Turn," no matter who sings it. Let us fan our frustration with the Star Mother to the point of fury; let us unleash this fury not just on her, but on anybody who has ever had a turn, on anybody who might still conceivably get one; let us blast the exclusive *system* of turns that represents us only peripherally, or vicariously, or not at all. And after we have done so much, let us acknowledge that the entire list of our grievances scarcely contains a single point not also expressed by "Rose's Turn," whose truth thus overcomes its alienation in the Star Mother's hypocritical self-appropriation and returns to us, fully proven, as our own. Hence, inasmuch as we must resent the Star Mother, we can't help culling to our heart the Rose who, in the "Turn"'s strangest twist of all, expresses just such resentment. Even earlier, when Rose's overbearing relation to the other characters bore a striking enough resemblance to the Star's pride of place among the other performers, it was impossible to reconcile the authority of a tried-and-true Broadway belter with the essentially compensatory bossiness of a stage mother. Now, with even that brand of power gone, Rose has become the pure negation of the Star who plays her. "When is it my turn? Don't I get a dream for myself?" As she poses these questions, wholly aware of their hopeless answers, not only is Momma Rose not a Star; unable to presume on that easy, almost automatic access to the musical stage which, in *Gypsy,* the feminine gender has consistently guaranteed, she can hardly be a Woman. And though in this sense Momma was never a Woman (a symbolic condition that *mère* Merman signified no less memorably in her name than in her famously sexless acting), here, having just been fired by Gypsy, she no longer remains even a Mother, with the maternal capacity to suckle the performance of others. Neither Star nor Woman nor Mother, then, who or what *is* Rose in "Rose's Turn"? Nobody and nothing at all, some people might say, referring the shadow of nervous breakdown that now darkens over her to the default of not just these, but all determinations of identity. But some people can't possibly be ourselves, who have had good reason to observe, of Star, Woman, and Mother alike, how regularly *Gypsy* partners these figures against those others which are, respectively, Wannabe, Man, and Child. The antitheses seem as ineluctable as they are inequitable: you either have it, as a term in the first series, or you've had it, as the corresponding term in the second. To eyes clairvoyantly sharpened on this binary logic, the voiding of stardom, femininity, and maternity in Rose must simultaneously grant her a precise, if strange, positive identity as well. "Rose's Turn" is in fact her metamorphosis, as staggering as any in Ovid, and one that she could not properly lament even if she had a mind to, for in beating her breast, she would strike no bosom, but only the shallow concavity into which it had been retracted, and in the effort to pull out her hair, it would prove too short for her grip; she might only scream, with a voice that had risen in pitch. In a word, "Rose's Turn" turns Rose into a boy, any one of the million male child wannabes grown pale and puny in their basement prisons, and whose futile, foreclosed perspective now howlingly commands the stage.

Momma's got to move, Momma's got to go · Though some people may find this phenomenon incredible, Laurents could hardly be more explicit in preparing for it, or Sondheim more dramatic in rendering it. Already in the heat of the quarrel that provokes the "Turn," the work of Rose's refashioning has evidently begun:

ROSE: Don't you take that tone to me. Your sister used to get that edge to her voice—
GYPSY: I am not June!
ROSE: You're not Louise either!
GYPSY: And neither are you!
ROSE: Oh yes I am! More than you, Miss Gypsy Rose Lee!

And the proposition here merely declared—that Rose *is* Louise, the Louise who hasn't yet become "Miss Gypsy Rose Lee"—is realized in the "Turn" proper, where Sondheim, never more spectacularly economical of means, reshapes Momma Rose into Boy Louise with the plasma of a single, but key word: "momma." No doubt, if Rose makes obsessive use of the word here, it is to name herself, in defiance of the child who no longer wants her in a maternal role. But eventually, just as if her mantric repetition had released the word into some psychic void, where it was free to feel the pull of a new gravity, she commits a fateful slip, which consists simply, but irrecoverably, in referring the word *to someone else*. This is, of course, her own mother, who left her in the same place she would later put Louise and the Star Mother has just put us: no place. "M-m-momma!" In the violence of that choking sound, the "Turn" completes the delirious fantasy, half-dream, half-nightmare, in which *Gypsy*'s thematics of male performance have always implicated the man engaging them: namely, that this Mother who is always having her say will vanish into the Boy whom she, or rather the form that enthrones her, has prevented from having his. Our murderous sentiments toward the Star Mother are not exactly exorcised in the unequaled enthusiasm with which, thus hailed by "Rose's Turn," we hail it in return. On the contrary, they may be the reason that, so long as a single piano bar is left standing, every already raging queen who intones the "Turn" there can be counted on to become as manic as if he were being pursued by Furies when he reaches those terrific last words: "This time for me."

V

Wherever we go, whatever we do · The Star Mother's last incarnation, in short, does nothing to resolve her crazy-making doubleness. As that thing of darkness one can only call Boy Rose, does she prove once more a Mother, having effaced herself so that *we* might have representation? Or do we feel all the more cruelly deprived of our voice now that hers is rendering what is, after all, merely our perspective? Between the adored mother who keeps a place for us and the resented monster who keeps it from us, "Rose's Turn" offers us neither reconciliation nor choice. Always the one and the other, the Star Mother calls us to the satisfactions of a close-binding that is never, in fact, close enough to satisfy. Small wonder that the aspiring young queen we have identified as Arnold, as Louise, as Pastey, and now finally as Rose herself, is a dizzy one, hardly knowing, even after this finale, where to turn:

> *She starts to follow* [as Gypsy goes off stage], *then turns back: The runway lights come on. She takes an eager step toward them, they go out in her face. A moment, then she turns and goes off.*

Only so, in the manner forecast by these two final turns, do we budge from the immobilizing melancholy in which this show of shows would otherwise place us. For just as no deprivation more bitterly frustrates us, so none more frequently urges us to relive it, than the one we tell ourselves might not have happened. "I could have been better than any of you." Hence, like Boy Rose, we *turn back* to the runway lights though we already know they will go out just when we reach them. We replay the *Gypsy* cast album as obsessively as a latter-day Confederate sympathizer might go over the Gettysburg campaign; indeed, as regularly as the fanatical devotion to a lost cause steeps *him* in all the minutiae of Civil War history, it turns *us* into genuine *Gypsy* scholars—the only ones, for that matter, the show has ever attracted. It is as if in endlessly retracing the course of our disappointment, we might still keep open those junctures where a different outcome still seemed possible, one on which, say, Arnold won the contest, or Louise became Tulsa's partner, or Rose, at the end of the "Turn," took off a wig. Hence, too, like Boy Rose, we *turn and go off,* in the Star Mother's train, to seek elsewhere, at some other show, the recognition that this one has almost but not quite given us. Failed by *Gypsy,* we cathect all the more tenaciously the musical stage per se, as the only place where we can hope to find a *Gypsy* "corrigé." The prospect, after all, is not absolutely impossible; who can say it will *never* turn up? But what regularly does turn up is the same *Gypsy* pattern in which the promise of recognition never even entails recognition of the promise, much less of its being broken. Our quest seems to get us no further than their trick "traveling step" takes the Newsboys when, against ever faster flickering lights, they give the impression of moving, but all that really passes is time.

·

She sends the big dipper a kiss · By 1966, for instance, some of us now shave—date improbable girls—cram for Latin exams, but the act remains essentially the same, with only the placard changed to read: *Mame.* As the Star Mother continues dominating the numbers to the point where she now takes over even the part of the man in the moon, her Boy, renamed Patrick, gets no more chance to blow his bugle (which in any case she has already appropriated for her own iconography on the playbill) than he did to ply his bellows when he was called Arnold. Yet we feel so alive again on reaching Beekman Place that it is hard after all not to think we have traveled a new highway to get here. Certainly, in the Woman to whom we still must entrust our desire for musical-theatrical expression, we find ourselves given spacious new accommodation, often so generous in fact as to leave her no more than a merely literal identity of her own. Whereas *Gypsy* allotted us a place only in the Star's necessarily discarded male past as Boy Louise or Schlepper Mazeppa, *Mame,* as if mischievously bent on reversing the notion that every gay man is "a woman inside," brings forth a world in which every woman must always seem to be harboring a gay man, a hidden, but scarcely secret agent who is ready at the drop of a hairpin to turn her into her own impersonator. As for hairpins, they fall in grateful profusion: when it is not Lawrence and Lee's book bidding us transpose female themes into a gay-male key ("Agnes, you're coming out!"), Herman's lyrics, with their own forays into queen's English, carry the principle right into the musical numbers, where some lines make sense in this key alone. What girl, now, would be likely to call the man in the moon "one of the girls"? Could the bitch who admits to having "dished" Mame be female at all? And the frankly mannish Vera who employs such language is only the most ostentatious signal of an all-inclusive camp in which, like the bougainvillea at the mention of her name, Mame too is apt to assume a sudden lavender hue. How should we mind, then, that the man in the moon is a lady, when the lady can hardly help simulating a guy in a gown?

What went wrong along the way? · The camp, too, only further indulges our affection for the Star Mother, which is perhaps nowhere else better returned. For if the Broadway stage never lets us become our Mother (however much it may make us want to), here our Mother gives us the next best thing by herself acting out our *gaminerie:* that's how young she feels! (Or rather that's why we feel she's young—why, likewise, we were no more bothered in the past when a grandmother played Peter Pan, than we will be in the future when another grandmother comes to impersonate Victor.) Yet this self-abnegating figure is never so much so that she yields her exclusive right to represent us; on the contrary, not for a moment does she cease being the required vehicle of a tenor whose *literal* expression, intolerable even here, continues to be thus preempted. Sooner or later, then, *Mame* must recognize the futility of a camp that cannot reduce Woman to mere place-holding without also exalting mere place-holding (which is infinitely more than we shall ever accomplish on this stage) to her most coveted privilege. Unsurprisingly, the recognition comes in the star turn, "If He Walked into My Life," which for all its tender sentimentality proves that Momma Mame is no anti-Rose, and in one respect may even be crueler than the latter in disenchanting our spellbound symbiosis with the Star Mother. For it is not just that, as in *Gypsy,* the Star Mother's claim that we have let her down rationalizes a majestically self-sufficient turn that leaves us out. Worse, as we hear Mame reproach herself for having "pampered"—"bossed"—at all events, produced the loving nephew who calls her "his best girl" and whom she considers "her big romance," we can't help knowing that her self-blame covers him in an even greater ignominy: it is the gay Patrick of connotation, not the snobbish Patrick of denotation, who causes her self-aggrandizing suffering, as if a rival "auntie" were unthinkable, or just thinkable enough to need to be, like our little Dixie Belles, put to shame. On the eventual immolation of this gay youth, Mame's youthful gaiety proves all along to have been feeding—or as she more delicately puts the point: "I never really found the boy before I lost him."

Will any person ever get the juice of you? · Delivered from Beekman Place, what do we do we now, what can we do but fall back into our traveling step? But at a certain moment, that step radically changes, from the creepmouse tread of solitary walkers to the martial stride of a uniformed brigade whose members, however light in the loafers, have finally put their foot down. And not the least thrill in being thus *en marche* is finding our kind (if not necessarily in the form of fellow travelers) everywhere emergent, even, in 1970, on the Broadway stage. The show of course is *Company,* where—no doubt because his selfish married friends insist on treating him like the maternal breast—a man called "Bobby bubi" has been allowed to step into the Star Mother's shoes. So many winks does Bobby share together with us that if we don't take this character for a gay cryptogram, it is only because there seems nothing cryptic about him. "Who is a flirt but never a threat?" Who is "the kind of guy most women want and never seem to get"? of whom they say, "Such a waste!"? These hoary social riddles are even less baffling when posed of "a person like Bob," who decorates his own apartment; escorts wives to the opera in place of their bored husbands; stays exactly the same while everyone else gets older; has an elective affinity for ladies who lunch; remains a bachelor because "not everyone should get married"; placates the married couple for his deviance with a charming manner while observing beneath it their every fault—have we forgotten anything? But as it happens, what flaws *Company* is not the obviousness of a homosexual stereotype (to which the power of the closet can sometimes

give polemical validity), but the incoherence of deploying it to de-
pict a heterosexual character. For as everyone knows, though his
profile so strongly resembles the Homosexual's before Stonewall,
and his dating game so pointedly refuses the heterosexual institutions of Marriage and the marriage-tracked Relationship, this
Bobby bubi is a Bobby bubba nonetheless. It is not just the characters in *Company* who all think so; in interview after interview, the
show's creators continue to put their authority behind the same
presumption, repudiating the possibility of gay representation with
an emphasis that couldn't be firmer if they were organizing a Saint
Patrick's Day Parade. We end up, then, falling into the same furious
incomprehension as Bobby's other girlfriends: we could understand
a person if a person was a fag, but if he is not, he must be as crazy
as he makes us.

Make me alive, make me confused · And ultimately his self-
contradiction extends to the show of which he is at the center.
Company has been called nasty for letting us gauge the exorbitant
narcissism of the married couples who demand that Bobby offer
them, in addition to endless material assistance, the philosophical
consolation of a psychopathology they can think of as worse than
their own. On the contrary, this spiteful-seeming vision is ipso facto
extraordinarily generous, since in adopting a perspective on the
couple that is not, for a change, the couple's own, it recognizes the
social existence of a whole ignored population of unmarried, not to
say unmarriageable, others. *Company* only becomes truly nasty with
Bobby's last number, when it writes off this perspective—and this
population—to become (in Sondheim's chillingly apt words) "the
most pro-marriage show in the world." As abruptly as if he were

knocked off his horse on the road to Damascus, Bobby finds himself testifying to the (social, psychological, sexual) rightness of the couple after all. But worse than the deus ex machina is the psychological realism meant to make it less crude. Nothing so ridiculous here as the joy of an instantaneous conversion; more plausibly, Bobby must suffer the anguish of a cure whose promised end is nowhere in sight—indeed whose only present measure is how desperately the patient wants to want what he still *can't* want, but has only been brought to concede that he *should*. "Being Alive" could hardly be more repugnant to watch if, instead of prodding Bobby with bits of psychobabble, his married friends gave him electric shocks while he looked at pictures of naked men; the number does nothing but enact the ruthlessness of a marital regime intolerant of the very exceptions by which, in fact, it has just been shown to live. Nor are we especially cheered by the fact that we have company—increasing and increasingly mixed—in this opinion of *Company*'s double-dealing, for it is the kind that only misery could love.

Daddy, I would love to dance · As we travel on, and the identity that had been prophesied long ago in the basement assumes increasing public visibility, *A Chorus Line* (1975) is what we'll remember for being the first musical to manifest the male fantasy that all the preceding ones (while no less essentially ministering to it) had maintained in secrecy. "I don't know why," Paul tells Zach, for whom he is auditioning, "but I loved musicals," and for once the musical stage lets one of the thousands of men who fill its ensembles go on to spell out what this phrase had to mean for him: that he loved imagining himself in the woman's place. It is, of course, supposed to be a "demeaning" experience when even this "terribly effeminate" boy who "was always being Cyd Charisse" actually finds himself there—in the drag review that is "the asshole of show business," and where one night, to make the abasement absolute, he is found in Anna May Wong costume by his no longer unsuspecting father. But the intensity of Paul's shame in the encounter is only matched by that of his pleasure, since, instead of the expected dressing-down, his father offers him an unprecedented love token:

> PAUL: He turned to the producer and he said, 'Take care of my son . . .' That was the first time he ever called me that . . . I . . . ah . . . I . . . ah— (*Paul breaks down*)

And the same delicious tale is repeated in the very telling of it, as Zach, shaken from aloofness by Paul's unmanly breakdown, comes on stage to put an arm around his shoulder. Pastey finally gets to strip and, still more wonderful, Cigar likes it!

Look, my eyes are dry · Yet *A Chorus Line* is no less intent on censoring this fantasy than on bringing it out. Paul's accident is no accident, but a strictly lame excuse for the necessity of ensuring that his Turn never comes. Homosexual fantasy may take the shape of a narrative memory or even a dramatic incident, but it must never assume what is, in the musical theatre, the far more involving and hence more dangerous form of a number. Or rather, insofar as it does so, it must have explicitly ceased to identify itself either as "homo" or as "sexual." In the first case, it becomes "The Music and the Mirror," where even before Paul's monologue—and despite his "fabulous extensions"—the chance to come through as Zach's Charisse has already been given to Cassie. In the second, it becomes

"One," whose thrilling combination of, on the one hand, the near-perfect homogeneity of the chorus line (in which even the girls wear top hats) and, on the other, our much moved fellow-feeling in watching it, could not more cruelly exemplify Freud's claim that what is crushed as homosexual desire stands proud as homosocial "esprit de corps." "Break a leg," we customarily tell performers to wish them luck; that Paul's injured knee expressly literalizes this dictum illustrates just how unabashed the show is prepared to be in bashing Paul for *its* own good. And to judge the success of Zach's show by that of Michael Bennett's, the sacrifice works like the charm it is meant to be: the rest of the troupe will step-kick-kick their way through 6,137 performances, not counting touring and stock. It is rumored (perhaps falsely, but certainly in keeping with the spirit of *A Chorus Line*) that Zach's cast dedicated their opening night performance to Paul, "who couldn't be on stage with us this evening, but whose example has inspired us all." And from his seat in the front row, bearing a cane of only the orthopedic sort, Paul thought: Shit.

We are what we are · Whether by *Gypsy* or *Mame,* by *Company* or *A Chorus Line,* our desire for the Star Mother's place has been treated to the same teasing disappointment. Not only is it always being excited without ever being fulfilled; even the articulation it receives *as* desire is exclusively the implicit, "subtextual" kind that, however abundant, will always be ignored whenever convenient, leaving us with nothing but another reason to sing along through our tears: that's Broadway. Obviously, the frustration of such unrecognized recognition no more inhibits a passionate attachment to the shows just named, which number among our cult's most visited shrines, than it did one to the similarly secret "best

friend" of our adolescence. Just so, in fact, out of a tantalizing possibility that may never be realized, but is never withdrawn either,
this obsessive cult is born. But encouraged (some people would say
spoiled) by a subculture whose flowering has at last satisfied *other*
ancient longings, we are also a bit weary of our *Gypsy*-driven pere-
grinations from one closet drama to another; even now, in 1983,
will they never cease? By way of an answer, we get a limousine (for
after so many years of imposed frugality our expenditures have
become extravagant all around) to drive us to a musical that, for
the first time in Broadway history, dares call itself gay. Here indeed,
entranced by the first-act finale, we dream that we are at last
watching the show of our dreams: a show that, unlike *A Chorus Line,*
lets a man perform in the Star Mother's place (where, just as she
would have done, he stops the show) and that, unlike *Company,* understands that such a man is more apt to wear the plumose regalia
of a drag queen than the wracked looks of the heterosexual convert
who sings "Being Alive." Nor is this all: in breaking with past tradition, the same number (unmistakably modeled on "Rose's Turn")
comes to fulfill it. No mere novelty, its transvestism finally expli-
cates the profound truth both of the "Turn" and of the whole fantasmatic relation of men to the musical that has been compacted in
the "Turn." Having been driven underground for as long as we can
remember (into a basement, a subculture, a subtext), this truth
herewith rises up to find public rehabilitation on the Broadway
stage. So what if the show is very forties and not a bit New Wave;
before the blissful vision it allows us to entertain, how could we not
have the evening of our life?

And what we are is an illusion · Sooner or later, though, we
must open our eyes; we have only arrived at *La Cage aux folles,* a

show whose success in bringing out the Broadway musical is in-
versely proportionate to its eagerness to be merely a "gay version"
of it. For the two things must prove quite different, even opposite
projects. When two or three gypsies come out during the course of
A Chorus Line, the show's liberal-sounding message could not ring
louder: "Yes, some gypsies do happen to be gay, just as some happen to be Puerto Rican, Asian, or black; your acceptance should
extend to all these minorities." But the unflinching disclosure that
as many as *three* of the men auditioning for Zach are gay is hardly
less fanciful than the naive idea, which it pretends to counter, that
none would be. What it really counters, of course, is the widely
suspected fact that, where the chorus of a Broadway musical is concerned, gay men do not form a minority at all, and even the true
minorities are likely also to be in this same majority. Three gypsies
come out so that *the chorus as a whole* may remain in the closet. Not
dissimilarly, the theme of homosexuality in *La Cage* works against
recognizing the homosexualizing fantasmatic structure of the
Broadway musical in general. While the structure is seducing any
man engaged by it into a feminine identification, the theme moves
to deny this identification by confining it within, precisely, a "cage"
of extreme cases. That gay men are hardly more likely than straight
to recognize themselves in Albin/Zaza suggests just how truly impossible this queen is intended to be. What is distancing, of course,
is not her transvestism—a drag queen is exactly what every man
watching a musical is led to want to be. If anything too close for
comfort, her transvestism is what is *distanced,* given an all but lunar
remoteness by the normal standards that the show's unperverted
sense of humor upholds throughout her characterization. Of every
joke, her difference from "us," *hypocrites spectateurs,* is the reassur-

ing, positively flattering point; by failing to butter her masculine toast, she butters our crusty masculinity instead. And since she thus spares us from having to recognize the strength of our desire to be *like* her, we are happy enough to grant her in return our glibbest tolerance, compassion, admiration, even affection. In *Company,* it was the disturbing specificity of our desire for a Turn that required repudiation: "Being Alive" sought to prove that a man might be the Star Mother without departing from—indeed, while in the very act of complying with—the most normative heterosexuality. *La Cage* works to disclaim the equally disturbing generality of that desire, which it suggests can only be the wish of outrageous—and hence (despite Herman's rhyme) not at all contagious—*folles.* Wilier than *A Chorus Line,* this "gay musical" denies its homosexualizing tendencies not by rejecting the homosexual, but by recognizing him, as a mythological creature that no one could ever actually be. And besides, now that those of us with a taste for the outrageous are used to gratifying it at some more truly mad extravaganza—to which we will in fact adjourn soon after the show—who would want to?

There are milestones, there are millstones · Nonetheless, our stride is broken; as if suddenly hobbled, it lurches to a standstill. Undistinguished on every other score except, perhaps, the score itself, *La Cage* marks that momentous pass in our travels, that impasse, where we no longer have a direction to give our progress, or even a destination to imagine for it. We would gladly put this disappointing show behind us, but as it also happens to be the goal we thought we were seeking, we hardly know to where we might move on (our uncertainty in this respect being rapidly annexed to a deep general despair as well, for a plague that prevents many of us from going anywhere, and discourages us all from hazarding long distances, has just appeared in our midst). To be sure, in the middle ground before us, we descry a land called *Falsettos* where, under a more conscientious administration, the tired old inmates of *La Cage* are said to be permitted the yard-exercise of a reinvigorating modern march. But what little curiosity we feel to visit the place is strictly touristic; despite the familiar faces we expect to encounter—all stamped with the same gay identity to which we have entrusted our own politics, ethics, sex lives—we cannot hope, or even wish, to make it home. For already from here we see that that identity too stands in an essentially reductive relation to the desire on which it is based: a kind of homogenous precipitate that can never in itself suggest how variously such desire continues to determine the density, color, taste of the whole richly embroiled solution out of which, in so settled a state, only a small quantity of it has fallen. However improved over *La Cage,* therefore, no gay musical is apt to elucidate what makes any musical gay; the featuring of homosexuals on the Broadway stage—even ones amicably drawn to our type—works positively against the recognition of the homosexual desire that diffuses through "other" subjects, objects, relations, all over the form. Indeed, by the contrary application of the same cruel logic, *Gypsy* and its closeted kind can now seem to have rendered a far richer account of this desire than anything we are likely to owe to a counter-tradition of gay avowal. After all, who that saw the closet at work on the musical stage, least of all ourselves, failed to witness this double operation: not only of "hiding" homosexual desire, but also of manifesting, across all manner of landscapes, an extensive network of hiding places—call them latencies—apparently ready-made for the purpose? To perceive the closet was always also to perceive the multitude of conditions under which closeting was possible, to glimpse, even as it was being denied, *the homosexual disposition of the world*. No doubt we like *La Cage* and its meager progeny even less for obliging us to admit, to our confusion, how keenly we miss this sublime vision, though it may have been the only truth that the closet's mendacity ever told.

Hey, L.A., I'm coming your way · Should we, then, reversing course, seek to reenter that dense cloud of obfuscation in which, albeit at our own mortifying expense, the true grandeur and extent of homosexual desire had been preserved, and where, at any rate, we would now be compensated for our invisibility not only with the old thrill of stumbling on obscure excitements, but also with the new, more deliberate pleasure of clarifying them? But the question is largely moot; if *La Cage* occupies the juncture in our travels at which we lose the desire to go forward, it may equally be said to indicate the point from which we have lost the ability to return, since in the aftermath of this show (justly regarded as the last successful "old-fashioned musical"), Broadway is as unlikely to produce the musical of our memories as it is unable to realize the musical of our dreams. The cliché proves exact: musicals aren't made "that way" any more (when indeed they are made at all). As with an old factory building converted into a shopping mall or a museum of its former life as a cannery or a cotton mill, the peculiar labor whose ring once pervaded the Broadway stage is no longer being accomplished there—or rather, to the extent that it still is (for relics of the old machinery have been preserved, occasionally maintained in working order), it is a half-hearted, trivial token of its formerly vital importance. It is not of course that, in the wake of Stonewall, homosexual desire had gradually ceased to be a general, even fundamental phenomenon of mass culture, and was now strictly confined to the new-born creatures called *gays*. Nor is it even that the musical spectacles of mass culture had stopped elaborating, indulging, and closeting a homoerotically charged fantasy, wistful and aggressive by turns, of taking the Star Mother's performing place. But in one sense at least, the shows that thematized homosexuality from *Company* through *La Cage* managed to "out" the Broadway musical after all. They may not have carried out the universal recognition we had longed for, but they did register, if only in their ostentatiously aversive relation to that longing, its increasing pressure (which seemed to build up internally quite as much as it did from an openly gay public), and so made the usual universal *nonrecognition* a more costly business. The budgets of *Gypsy* and *Mame,* for instance, had never needed to include the camouflage of fag jokes à la *Company* or the gay-bashing of *A Chorus Line.* Hence, like a multinational that, alarmed by the soaring costs of manufacture in North America, decides to move its factories to Mexico or Southeast Asia, where it may exploit cheaper labor with less fuss too, so mass culture, when it could no longer help sensing that the Broadway mu-

Who's got the pain? (reprise) · Jack Klugman (the original Herbie): "Something else I'll never forget: we were three weeks into rehearsal and we were at the Amsterdam Theatre, and Steve and Jule came in very late and announced that they'd just finished 'Rose's Turn.' We stopped the rehearsal and Jule sat down at the piano and played it, and Steve got up and sang it with such feeling and such awareness of what it was about that I just fell apart. When Steve did 'M-m-momma, M-m-momma,' and couldn't get it out, Ethel and I just burst into tears" (Craig Zadan, *Sondheim & Co.,* New York: Harper & Row, 1989, p. 46).

sical was "a gay thing," reconsigned its long-standing investment in
the form to musical spectacles that were better at preserving the
collective innocence—or just more efficient at enforcing the collective ignorance—of the nature of the job they had taken over. In
other words, supposing that, in our retreat from *La Cage,* we did
seek to rediscover *Gypsy's* fantasmatics of performance envy in cul-
turally vital form, we would have to *leave the Street*—perhaps for
the screen of Disney animation, on which a new generation of artists, together with an old team of musical songwriters, has reincar-
nated the Star Mother as, well, a witch, given to consoling the Poor
Unfortunate Souls whose voice she has appropriated and on whose
very substance her oversized figure seems to have battened; or
even, in the opposite direction, for the scene of Heavy Metal,
where the strutting is so "heavy" indeed that there needs all the
homophobic belligerence here allowed—a lot more than on the
"nice" Broadway stage—to disguise the family resemblance between Momma Rose and, say, her finally triumphant bastard Axl.

A wonderful dream · Yet since no one who worshipped in
the Broadway cult during its glory days would dream of abandoning
it for a modern service—he would sooner wear a turned-around
baseball cap or pierce his lip—we may no more advance thus side-
ways than forward or back. Our only possible move, in fact, has
been down: to sink ever more deeply into nostalgia, the dank
nether world where the waning of a cult, of their belief that it will
deliver them, commonly sends its diminished members. Haunted
with the shades of departed stars and shows, not to mention spectators, this is the country that, as scripture says, "we've covered . . .
like Gypsies." (Like any other self-respecting fortune-teller, *Gypsy*

told our future in riddles that would become plain only after what they prophesied had come to pass, so that no boy among us, however much he first puzzled, or then marveled over the multiple meanings of the show's title, ever imagined that "gypsy" might designate the one that was being permanently put in his soul.) No doubt, in the musty air here we catch a second wind, and on the mushy soil our step recovers some old vigor. Yet the difference must be palpable between the basement of our childhood (though also close and damp) and this new underground, where our youthful passions "live on"—beyond their freshness—to sprout a sentimental or pedantic mold, and where they must not only seem, but also, finally, become as false as dancers whose overready smiles attempt to cover up a sloppy routine, or else who, to the perfectly remembered execution of intricate steps, have given up their heart. Sometimes, though (perhaps during the night after one of the well-named "revivals" we regularly attend), we dream that, far from embalming it, the fetishistic attentions we pay to the Broadway musical end in exploding it, in launching high into the cultural ethos all those "homo" energies that, even during its prime, never circulated so freely as they now spiral out from a retrospection that is thus releasing them not "once again," but *for the first time*. And we dream on that, with this explosion, in the rubble of fragments that makes fertile ground for bricolage of all kinds, the scattered corpse of the Broadway musical starts to acquire that property of life which consists in "taking a turn," a turn that might well—oh, the compulsion is incurable!—serve our own. But in this dream, of course, we have passed the age of being sure we believe; like certain agnostics, we content ourselves with following in the old way, as if that fidelity were the only faith we had left.

Acknowledgments

And why? Some guy • I owe my first idea for these pages to Randy Cooper, and my first desire to write them to Tas Shaughnessy. *Santa Claus is sitting here* • That Arthur Laurents gave me the heady opportunity to talk about *Gypsy* with its author implies only his considerable kindness, not an endorsement of my dramatic reading of his work. *Dreamgirls* • Of the many who kept my fantasy alive during a long gestation, I thankfully mention: the late Marston Anderson, Lawrence Benn, Leo Bersani, Herschel Bowles, Anne Anlin Cheng, the late Raul Companioni, Carol T. Christ, Suzanne Daly, Sandy Drooker, Adam Feldman, Philip Fisher, Stephen Friedman, Catherine Gallagher, Michael Gallant, Amanpal Garcha, Stephen Greenblatt, Robert Lambert, Joseph Litvak, Jeffrey Masten, Richard Meyer, Ida and Hank Miller, Franco Moretti, Laura Mullen, Mary Ann O'Farrell, Michael Perelman, David Pickell, Elaine Scarry, Bart Saint Clare, and the late John Wolski. *Kimi to boku to wa* • The Japanese language displays a feature of which, in my purely imaginary relation to it, I am inordinately fond. This is *aizuchi,* a kind of "enthusiastic listening" in which your conversation partner accompanies your discourse with a continuous counterpoint of encouraging interjections. The beauty of aizuchi (or its charity) is that, however your words may vary in merit, a labor of affection and intelligence will regularly return them to you as having the most extraordinary interest. Yet still more agreeable than this fiction, I think, must be the grain of truth lodged within it, for who performing thus assisted would not surpass himself in fact? Though this essay owes Lee Edelman a million things, it is dedicated to him for just one: his great fluency in Japanese.

San Francisco

Illustration Credits

p. 5: courtesy of Zenith archive.

pp. 10, 15, 18, 25: from the author's collection.

p. 33: Michael Perelman, *At the Palace*, oil on canvas, 20" x 20", 1996.

p. 42: Michael Perelman, *Only the Lonely*, oil on canvas, 18" x 18", 1996.

p. 52: Michael Perelman, *Rose's Turn*, oil on canvas, 24" x 24", 1996.

p. 61: Michael Perelman, *Stormy Weather*, oil on panel, 24" x 24", 1994.

p. 67: Billy Rose Theatre Collection, Friedman-Abeles Collection, The New York Public Library for the Performing Arts, Astor, Lenox and Tilden Foundations.

p. 85: Billy Rose Theatre Collection, Friedman-Abeles Collection, The New York Public Library for the Performing Arts, Astor, Lenox and Tilden Foundations.

p. 97: Martha Swope, © Time Inc.

p. 135: Billy Rose Theatre Collection, Friedman-Abeles Collection, The New York Public Library for the Performing Arts, Astor, Lenox and Tilden Foundations.

Lightning Source UK Ltd.
Milton Keynes UK
UKHW011249060219
336838UK00005B/254/P